THE PRESS AND ITS READERS

THE PRESS
AND
ITS READERS

A report prepared by

MASS OBSERVATION

for

THE ADVERTISING SERVICE GUILD

faber and faber

This edition first published in 2009
by Faber and Faber Ltd
Bloomsbury House, 74–77 Great Russell Street
London WC1B 3DA

Printed by CPI Antony Rowe, Eastbourne

A CIP record for this book is available from the British Library

ISBN 978-0-571-25193-3

CONTENTS

THE PROBLEM

THE researcher into the power and popularity of the British Press has hitherto been more concerned with the subject as it affects either the politician or the newspaper advertiser. In the political world there has always been much speculation on the importance of the Press to the fortunes of political parties, and social science has been encouraged to examine this influence. More recently, as newspaper readership became almost universal, the newspaper in addition to its presentation of news and views has had to regard itself as a medium of commercial and industrial advertising. The advertiser, called on to pay higher prices as circulations mounted, began to get more and more curious as to the precise nature of the circulation he was buying.

Thus there have been successive attempts to analyse circulations by age, social class and sex.

It is perhaps surprising that while so much attention has been given to these two aspects of the Press, little attention has been given to the study of *attitudes* of readers to their newspapers. Without some clear idea of these reader attitudes neither the politician nor the business man can make any proper assessment of the Press. We therefore feel that this Report is, in a sense, a pioneering one and will be of some significance to others besides the sociological student. We have not thought it necessary to offer any cut-and-dried list of conclusions to which the reader might be irresistibly drawn. The subject does not lend itself to easy simplification.

There are, however, one or two explanatory notes to be offered by way of preface. The difficulties of book production today inevitably cause a gap between the field work of a report and its final appearance in type. A few of the topics which are therefore reflected in the evidence may sometimes appear to be a little out of date and possibly a little out of tune with the news of the day in which this survey must be read. This lag is inevitable, but it does not invalidate the work as a whole. Circulations have risen during the course of publication, for more newsprint has led to bigger sales; but we have no reason to believe that the rise in circulations has made any material change in the complexion of our findings. The basic factors of taste, choice and attitude remain, and changes in circulations are only expressions of these.

References are made to the quantitative surveys of circulation, particularly to one which has recently been sponsored by the Hulton Press. To those who may wonder how much difference there is between these two methods of investigation there is one example which may be quoted. According to the Hulton figures the *News Chronicle* and the *Daily Express* have in effect much the same readership, assessed by class, sex and age. It will be seen later in this report that the papers are very dissimilar when viewed through the eyes of their readers and when the bare statistics of formal interviewing are clothed with the words and moods of the people behind the decimal point. It is this use and interpretation of research methods for which Mass-Observation stands, and in which it alone specializes.

Mass-Observation is interested in finding out what people really think and in sketching in a rounded picture that does not merely confine itself to percentaged results of what has been said in answer to certain formal questions.

Using statistics as a means rather than an end, Mass-Observation is concerned with the live dynamic whole of feeling and behaviour. This is the background against which the present investigation was undertaken and carried through, and it is in the same mood of human interest that the results of the survey are presented for publication.

As was to be expected, a good deal of pertinent comment has been made on the subject of how much influence the Press has on public opinion. While generalizations are dangerous to make on such an important subject as this, we think we have demonstrated that whatever that influence may be, it is essentially a long-term process. The ability of an editor to change the minds of his readers is nothing like so dominant or so certain as that of a shepherd and his dog at a sheep trial. There is much evidence to suggest that the actual prestige and influence of the Press has declined in inverse ratio to the rise in its circulation. The popularity of newspapers has gained import by the technique of flavouring news with the spice of sensation. While this may interest a reader, it does not encourage him to have a greater respect for the pages he reads. On such matters, editors themselves, and other experts of all sorts may disagree—or agree to differ. This report seeks to provide objective data which should help to lift some aspects of this important problem above the level of personal prejudice or facile debate. Few subjects are more important to the future of this democracy than the present influence and the future development of the popular (or unpopular) Press.

I: NON-READERS

'All I like is gangster stories, though there's precious little chance of reading here. Three rooms we got and three kids knocking around. No convenience, no nothing except water. I'm glad to get out of the house, I can tell you.' (*Factory worker.*)

This man said his favourite spare time occupation was drinking in the pub, and his desire to go out rather than stay at home reading is easily understood. His particular handicap is by no means uncommon; housing difficulties combined, as will be seen later, with inadequate education underlie much of the present day lack of interest in reading.

But it is impossible to discuss non-readers as if they were a single group. Some people read books but not papers, others read papers but not books; in particular they may read one kind of paper and more or less ignore others. *Our material does, in fact, show that although there is such a thing as a 'non-reader type' with fairly coherent background of habits, attitudes and outlook in a pattern of his own, there is considerable variation between the several different groups of non-readers.* People who do not read Sunday papers, for instance, are quite different to those who read no weekday papers. And non-readers of books, as a group, present yet another set of distinguishing characteristics.

Early in 1947, Mass-Observation made a National Survey of reading-habits, not just confined to newspapers.[1] Only 3 per cent of the general population said they never read anything at all, a figure that must be regarded as a minimum estimate in light of the shame people tend to feel in making such an admission. Such *total* non-readers were women rather than men, and appeared chiefly amongst the unskilled working-class and the over-forties. (It is only magazines that women read more than men.) Marriage increased the tendency *not* to read, even though size of family seemed to make little difference.

This picture of the type of person who reads nothing at all is also

[1] See Appendix I for details of this Survey.

roughly typical of the non-reader specifically of books. Our 1947 national sample figures showed that as many as one person in every three does not read books, and this group consists disproportionately of married people, women and the less well-off or less well-educated. In addition older people read books less than the young.

Newspapers

Non-reading of newspapers is much less common. 1948 Hulton Readership figures show that Sunday papers are read by all but 8 per cent of the population, and dailies by all but 13 per cent. Taking the non-readers of every kind of newspaper as a single group, the ways in which they differ from the non-readers of books become apparent. Although again women and the unskilled working-classes are most in evidence, this time it is the 16–20s, the group containing the *highest* proportion of book-readers, that reads newspapers *least* of all. Moreover (perhaps partly a reflection of this reverse trend), marriage decreases the tendency to read books at the same time as it increases newspaper reading. An explanation of this may well be that lack of time does in fact have an adverse effect on book-reading, and that, where this happens, newspaper reading is intensified as a sort of compensation.

But it has already been pointed out that the non-readers of Sunday and daily papers are really two quite distinct groups. *In particular, although working-class people read daily papers less than the better-off, on Sundays the non-reader is more likely to belong to the higher income groups.* Especially amongst men, it is the better-off who read Sunday papers least of all. Occupational differences illustrate this. According to Mass-Observation figures in the present survey, domestic and catering workers show the *lowest* proportion not reading Sunday papers, and the *highest* proportion not reading dailies. Professional and business people, on the other hand, the group with the highest average income, read Sunday papers least of all.

Outlook and Interests

But apart from the groups from which they are drawn, there is another difference between the weekday and the Sunday non-reader. In the present Mass-Observation Survey, people were asked to rate their degree of interest in a wide range of subjects and activities, and the results were related to newspaper reading. In almost every subject—in home activities and sport (both playing and watching), in politics, in pub-going and social activities, and in every form of cultural interest, even film and radio—non-readers of daily papers[1] include a disproportionate number of people with no interest at all. Only in religion and dancing were non-readers more interested than the average person, and only in 'club activities' were they equally interested. Another test gave similar results. In order to check on relative degrees of interest in three different aspects of life—sport, politics and light home news—people were asked whether they could remember who won last year's Derby, what government was in power in Jugoslavia, and who was George Neville Heath. In every case people with no interest in any particular daily paper were more ignorant than others.

Another indication of the general apathy of the weekday non-reader, arose from our earlier National Survey of reading habits. People who did not read daily papers also tended to read books less than average, and spent less than the normal amount of time listening to the wireless and drinking; instead, one in four, an unusually high proportion, had 'no particular' spare time occupation, or spent their leisure in less individualistic activities such as the cinema and theatre, dancing, visiting, etc. Very few of them, moreover, belonged to Trade Unions or other organizations. A much earlier survey in 1941 also showed that non-readers were considerably less than normally interested in the news.

The non-reader of Sunday papers, on the other hand, presents quite a different picture. When members of this group were questioned on their interest in the subjects about which weekday non-

---

[1] The term 'non-reader' *here* is only an approximation to fact. The question used was 'Which do you like best (of the daily morning papers)?' since the main object was to discover the relation between newspaper preference and personality type. People who answered 'none' are for the most part non-readers, but some may merely be disillusioned and cynical newspaper readers.

readers had been so apathetic, they emerged with an above-average inclination for the more serious and intellectual interests. *As a group, people who do not read Sunday papers are more than usually interested in politics, foreign affairs, reading, social work, religion and classical music.* In everything else—in sport, films, dancing, pub-going, etc.—they are below average in their interest. *In short, the Sunday non-reader is precisely the opposite type of person to the non-reader of weekdays: he is most concerned with the more serious interests and activities,* the very ones which have little appeal to people who do not read daily papers. Later it will be seen that the Sunday papers tend to be read with a totally different purpose to that of the weekday reader; their development is towards feature and gossip rather than more serious news, and it seems likely that it is just this development that leads the Sunday non-reader to avoid the paper. Daily paper non-readers, on the other hand, tend to be apathetic and ill-informed, and their lack of interest is a negative, not a positive, feeling. Perhaps for that very reason they are a much more promising potential source of circulation increase than the non-readers of Sunday papers, who have definite interests that the papers leave unsatisfied.

Why They Don't Read

So far as the non-reader of daily papers is concerned, it would seem that he keeps away from newspapers out of an apathy that characterizes almost all his activities. But what does the non-reader himself give as his reason? One explanation which has already been suggested (though this applies even more to the non-reader of books) is inadequate housing. But reasons for not reading at all often sound suspiciously like rationalization. Most common of all is scarcity of time; after this, in order of frequency, come fatigue, lack of interest, bad sight and a complete or partial inability to read. The fact that size of family has no apparent effect on reading seems particularly to suggest that many of these reasons are more of an excuse, and that lack of interest is the more fundamental cause. Lack of interest is closely associated with inadequate education, and the influence of both factors can be seen in comments such as these, taken from our 1946 survey of book-reading in Tottenham:

'I'm not very good at reading, I never was. I've never liked it, somehow.' (*Retired man, unskilled working class.*)

'I really don't get interested in books, somehow. It means going out to get them.' (*Gas-fitter, aged* 40.)

Others have found more interesting ways of spending their leisure:

'There's such a lot of things I'd rather do if I got the time.' (*Young man, factory worker, likes to spend his spare time at the dog track.*)

But for the most part the strongest impression given by people who have no interest in books is that *they have never learnt properly to read*. To some, for instance, reading is a task rather than a relaxation, and something that can only be expected of other people. *It is in this respect particularly that newspapers often have an advantage over books:*

'I don't read books, only papers. Books take too long. I can never remember what's happened before if I stop once.' (*Builder, aged* 35.)

Each of the reasons so far given for not reading books also apply to newspapers, although the time, fatigue and interest factors may often mean that newspapers are read in place of other, 'heavier' reading matter. But there are other reasons as well why people do not read newspapers; one is money. Already it has been seen that people of lower income groups read daily papers less than the better-off, but Sundays as much, or more—a fact that, as will be shown later, may partly be a reflection of the higher magazine-gossip interest of the latter, but may also indicate that regular daily expenditure is too much. Even in Mass-Observation's middle-class Panel, in which average weekly income is about £11 10s., one man says he cannot afford daily papers:

'I don't feel like wasting the money—it adds up. I glance at odd papers, buy a Sunday paper, and the local weekly rag, and listen to the BBC news instead.'

On the other hand weekly rather than daily reading may sometimes be entirely a matter of lack of time during the working week:

'I don't take any daily papers but I take one on Sundays. I don't have time to read the dailies in the morning, so it's not much use my having them, is it? I like Sunday papers, though. You can read all the news of the week in them. I take a lot because I like to read both sides, see.' (*Miner, aged* 30.)

Sometimes, however, disapproval of daily papers seems to outweigh lack of interest:

'I don't read a paper unless somebody happens to have it. I don't buy a newspaper—it's a lot of piffle anyway. Never buy a paper. . . .' (Why?). . . . 'When you read a paper, you think this is a Tory paper, or a Labour paper, you never get the news straight. Now I think they ought to give it to you unbiased. Like say a magistrate says something, the journalist adds a bit, saying he thinks the sentence was fair or something like that.' (50-*year-old café proprietor, ex-boxer.*)

In the larger towns, evening papers often replace the National dailies, particularly amongst the people who are short of reading time until the evening, or who want to read only the sort of news that the evening paper provides. And evening papers are sometimes read hardly in the normal newspaper sense:

'I don't have a daily paper. I buy the *Evening News*, because I can't get a *Radio Times*, and I want the wireless programmes.' (*Middle-class woman, 28, book-shop assistant.*)

As this report proceeds, more light will be thrown on the vital question of how much interest the reader shows in the newspaper, how thoroughly he reads it, and which parts he buys it for. Until this is done, discussion of the non-reader cannot be complete. But even without this further material, it is quite clear that there are two types of non-readers. One predominates amongst the group that does not read dailies, and the key-point to his character is lack of interest; the other, appearing chiefly among non-readers of Sunday papers, refrains from reading not because he has no interest in the news, but, on the contrary, because his outlook is more than normally serious and the Sunday paper does not give him what he wants. A not inconsiderable group is in the position of the Essex man who said he did not read any Sunday paper because:

'They are a rehash of old news, sensational subjects couched in the best journalese, and I don't like any of them.' (*Artisan, aged* 24.)

II: WHO READS WHAT?

The Hulton Surveys

IT would be impossible to write about readership of the Press without some reference to the Hulton Readership Surveys that were conducted in early 1947 and early 1948. These were two surveys made over the whole of Great Britain by the method of quota sampling, designed to give some broad statistical measure of readership according to age, sex, domestic status and class groups.

The value of these measures lies not only in the positive information made available but also in the contradiction of certain popular misconceptions. Some of the main implications about the readership of the national daily and Sunday papers that arise from a study of the Hulton Survey of 1948 are briefly summarized in the following tables:

Readership by Sex

TABLE I

Papers with a Significant Predominance of Readership among Men

The Times	Daily Herald	Reynolds News
Daily Express	News Chronicle	Empire News

Paper with a Significant Predominance of Readership among Women

Daily Graphic

Papers with a Fairly Even Distribution of Readership Among Both Sexes

Daily Mirror	Daily Telegraph	Daily Mail
News of the World	People	Sunday Pictorial
Sunday Express	Sunday Dispatch	Sunday Chronicle
Sunday Graphic	Sunday Times	Observer

Readership by Age Group

TABLE 2

Papers with a Significant Predominance of Readers under 45 years of age

Men	Women
Daily Mirror	Daily Mirror
Sunday Pictorial	Sunday Pictorial
Daily Worker	News of the World
	Empire News
	Reynolds News

Papers with a Significant Predominance of Readers over 45 years of age

Men	Women
News Chronicle (over 65)	News Chronicle (over 65)
Daily Graphic	Daily Graphic
The Times (over 65)	Daily Mail
Sunday Chronicle	Sunday Chronicle
Daily Telegraph (over 65)	Daily Telegraph
Sunday Times (over 65)	Sunday Times
Observer (over 65)	Observer

Readership by Class

Analysis of readership by class is significant only in so far as reliance can be placed on the definition of class and the allocation of informants to certain classes. If the broad classification of those with incomes above and below £400 a year be taken, then certain trends in readership can be found.

TABLE 3

Papers with a Significant Predominance of Readership Within the Upper Income Group

The Times	Daily Telegraph	Sunday Express
Daily Mail	Daily Graphic	Sunday Times
Observer		

Papers with a Significant Predominance of Readership Among the Lower Income Group

Daily Mirror	Daily Herald	News of the World
People	Sunday Pictorial	Empire News

III: READERS OBSERVED

ONE way of finding out what people read in the newspaper is to watch them reading. For this reason, Mass-Observation investigators observed people in public library reading rooms,[1] in trains and buses and in the street, and noted the length of time spent on each paper, on each page of the paper, and on each main item. A record was made of the order in which each paper was read, and, as often as possible, the headings of all items turned to were also recorded, so that later analysis could discover which sorts of news and which sorts of presentation gained most and least attention.

In libraries the average reader spends four to five minutes on each daily paper that he reads. Least time is given to the picture papers, the *Daily Graphic* and the *Daily Mirror*, with slightly under $3\frac{1}{2}$ minutes. In trains and buses, on the other hand, rather longer is spent on the paper, with an average of about 6 minutes; but here time is likely to be strongly influenced by the length of the journey. *Evening papers* on transport receive even more prolonged attention; 8 minutes, on average, is spent on each. It seems likely that train and bus readers spend longer on their paper than readers in the public library (although it must be remembered that the latter may go on to read another paper after the first one timed); and that evening papers are read more thoroughly than morning papers.

Similar material (but this time not confined to public library and transport observation) emerged from an earlier Mass-Observation

[1] Newspaper reading in public libraries is in many ways quite different from newspaper reading in the home. In particular it is unlikely to provide reliable indications of the relative popularity of individual papers, and the actual time spent on each paper may well be different to that of home reading. As a guide to the relative degrees of interest shown in each sort of *item*, however, as well as to reading habits and reading orders and the differences between papers in this respect, public library observations can be of great value. To some degree their importance can be gauged by the extent to which they are supported by material from other sources, a development which does, in fact, occur in this survey. There is, however, one big exception to this general comparison; the 'situations vacant' column of each newspaper, particularly *The Times* and *Daily Telegraph*, are given much more attention in public libraries than at home.

survey. Our 1946 study of book-reading in Tottenham, in the course of which 1,000 people were interviewed, showed that *Daily Telegraph* readers claim to spend the most time on newspapers every week, and *Daily Mirror* readers least.

What They Read

Which parts of the paper are read during this time? More detailed analysis of our public library material shows that most of the time is spent on reading the news, particularly the front page news. In the four-page popular papers nearly half the total time is spent on the front page, and three-quarters on the two news pages, first and third, together. Not quite a fifth is spent on the second page, with its feature articles and editorial, and only a tenth on the back page, mainly devoted to sport. Picture paper readers, on the other hand, devote less time to front page news and instead distribute their reading more evenly through the entire paper. In the *Daily Mirror*, for instance, the strip page is given as much attention as the second page features or page three of home news. People who read picture papers appear to be less interested in the news than readers of the more serious papers, but even so two-thirds of their reading time is spent on news as distinct from features and sport.

Some extracts from observers' accounts of public library readers will illustrate this difference between popular and picture papers:

Skilled working-class woman, aged 45. 'Picks up the *Daily Graphic* and looks at front page headlines. Reads "Woman Recluse 89 Dead in Trunk". Reads length of column—turns to back page and continues to read further column (as continued from front page) about the murder (Time 4 minutes). Reads column "Anne's Wedding, etc." (1 minute), back again to front page—reads column on extreme right "The Dyke", etc. Turns to centre pages, looks at pictures (another minute). Turns to page 2 and reads "Money is no object". Puts elbows on table. Also reads article on lower page 2 "20 years on your age" (5 minutes). Turns over to page 3—reads cartoon "Blondie". Looks up and sees that another woman has finished with magazine *Britannia and Eve*—leans over and takes it.'

Unskilled working-class man, aged 30. 'Picks up *Daily Mirror*, glances at front page news items (headlines only). Opens *Daily Mirror* to page 3 and reads cartoon—glances at remaining reading matter but doesn't settle down to read anything special. Turns to page 4—reads "Jane"—looks at pictures. Leaves *Daily Mirror* open centre page—walks away.'

And a popular paper:

A skilled working-man, aged 60. 'Wearing trilby hat, gloves, blue jacket, black striped trousers. Takes up *News Chronicle*. First spends 2 minutes skipping through whole contents of the front page, only reads thoroughly columns dealing with miners. Turns to second page and straight away reads readers' letters which are headed "Too Old at 47". This takes ½ minute. Spends the next ½ minute glancing through "Spotlight" by A. J. Cummings —this article headed "No Iron Dukes Now". Reads no more. Does not even glance at pages 2 and 3.'

In the London evening papers about a third of the total time is given to front page news, but relatively little to news on other pages. Gossip, features, and the sports pages, are the chief draw. In many ways, as will be seen later, interest in evening papers is more akin to that shown in Sunday rather than morning papers.

Analysis by item, rather than by page, again shows that morning paper readers are most of all inclined to look at the news; one-third of all the items that people were seen to read concerned political news, and a fifth home news items. On the other hand, this included the briefest headline reading and is unlikely to represent serious interest, especially since political news tends to appear on the front page so that it does not have to be specially turned to. One item in every six was a sporting item and one in every ten a picture. Feature articles made up a twelfth of all items looked at, and the remainder consisted of equally small proportions of gossip, editorial, letters and comics, including cartoons. (These generalizations cover non-pictorial papers only.) The following table shows how much people tend to concentrate on one sort of item:

TABLE 4

Average number of items of this sort looked at by popular paper eaders (excluding people in each case who do not read this sort of item at all)

	No. of items		No. of items
Political news	2·4	Editorial	1
Home news	1·8	Letters	1
Sports	1·6	Comics, cartoons	1
Gossip	1·2	Articles	1
Pictures	1·2	Adverts.	1

In other words, anyone who looks at political news items at all is likely to look at two or three, whilst anyone who looks at feature articles or gossip news at all is likely to look at one item only.

Lastly, what proportion of people read each sort of item? Again political news heads the list:

TABLE 5

Percentage of people reading daily papers who read items of this kind:

Item	%
Political news	58
Home news	45
Sports	42
Pictures	38
Articles	32
Gossip	9
Editorial	9
Letters	7
Cartoons and comics	7
Misc.	2

Rather more than half the people observed at least *glanced* at the political news, nearly as many looked at home news, and every second person read some sporting item or other. But the following extracts give an idea of the relative strength of interest that accompanies these readings.

A *Times* reader, for instance:

An artisan class woman, aged 45. 'Reads "Personal Column" then turns to the centre news page. Glances at the News Column "Czechoslovak Elections" —"British Resolutions for Palestine"—scans the headlines in general (1½ minutes), then turns to page 5. Looks as if she's interested in the correspondence, reads "Clothing Coupon Bonus" (time spent on page 5— 1 minute). Turns back to page 3—looks at various fashion adverts.— Debenham's, Harrods, and Barkers. Looks interested (time, 1 minute). Turns to page 7, looks at Derry and Toms advert. for coats, etc. Then scans headlines—"Court circular" (time spent on page 7—1 minute). Turns back to front page, glances down various columns of adverts.'

A *News Chronicle* reader:

'25-year-old middle-class man; side-whiskers, sports jacket, grey striped flannels. Turns straight away to "Spotlight" by A. J. Cummings, on page 2, glances through all this. Page 3—reads all the headlines quickly. Turns to back page; reads for one minute boxing columns on Freddie Mills. Turns

22

to page 3 again (investigator's view blocked here). Then to page 1—reads "Woman shot in Soho flat". Turns finally to page 2, reads readers' letters. Total time spent—5 minutes.'

And a *Daily Express* reader:

'55-year-old skilled worker, bald-head, glasses, shabby striped coat and blue trousers. First reads every headline on page 1 ($\frac{1}{2}$ minute). Turns to page 2, reads all through editorial opinion (2 minutes), then Beachcomber's "By the Way". Glances through "Thinking Aloud". Looks at fashion picture. Starts on page 3—reads main headlines and various sentences in the text at random. Then turns to page 4, and reads "Dick Turpin Shocks Vince Hawkins" (sport). Glances through Frank Bulten's article, then goes. Total time spent—7 minutes.'

On the whole, although the majority of people look at the political news, it is only to glance at it. Relatively few ignore it completely, but on the other hand equally few show signs of any real interest in it. And although most of people's reading time, in so far as dailies are concerned, is devoted to news, it is largely the sort of home news that is partly gossip, and that has an easy personal appeal.

IV: READERS TESTED

An easier way of observing people is to get them to watch themselves. Working along these lines we set a practical test to members of Mass-Observation's National Panel,[1] designed to discover which part of the paper had made the most impression on them. In July 1947, a sealed envelope was sent to each Panel member with instructions that it should be opened last thing in the evening of July 16th. Having opened it members were asked to write down what they could recall reading in the morning paper of that day. A similar experiment was carried out on Sunday papers. Results are interesting in that they show how newspapers are read by people who are likely to be interested in the more serious parts of the news; though representative only of the interests of the more intelligent of the middle-class, they illustrate news consciousness where it exists at a more than usually interested level.

Daily Papers

The day chosen for the experiment was Wednesday, July 16th, 1947, a day on which the newspapers were headlining Arthur Deakins' suggestion of the possibility of direction of labour, E. Arnot Robertson's libel action, an announcement by Strachey on rationing changes, the Paris Aid to Europe Conference, Princess Elizabeth and her fiancé dancing in Edinburgh, more cases of infantile paralysis, and the results of a Middlesex v. Leicester cricket match.[2]

Of every 100 readers of national morning papers (of whom readers of the *News Chronicle*, *Daily Telegraph* and *Times* accounted for more than half), a third were able at the end of the day spontaneously to

[1] Mass-Observation's National Panel is a predominantly middle-class group, and one which has proved itself to be considerably more serious in its interests, and more socially inclined than the average person.

[2] These news items are selected arbitrarily, as varying types of news items given importance (but not necessarily the *most* importance) on July 16th.

recall the Deakin announcement, and a similar proportion mentioned the Paris Talks. Rather more than a quarter of the group recalled the cricket results, and also the news concerning the E. Arnot Robertson libel suit. One in five mentioned Princess Elizabeth, and one in five the Strachey ration announcements. One in every ten remembered about the infantile paralysis cases.

Some people remembered in detail almost everything they had read; this 34-year-old Essex office-manager, for instance, was by no means unusual:

'I glanced at the front page of today's *Daily Mail* when I came downstairs and saw it on the hall table. I read the *News Chronicle* at breakfast between 8.30 and 8.45, and again at lunch between 1.30 and 1.55. I can't remember a word I read in the *Daily Mail*, but in the *Chronicle* there was: the libel action brought by E. Arnot Robertson. Arthur Deakin speaking on the direction of labour. The Queen had got something in her eye. A leader on newsprint. A leader on Strachey's jam announcement. A small cartoon "How did you know I'd been abroad?" Bevin saying the people of all nations wanted to agree. The "American Ranger" salvage case. Meat ration announcement. The name of the cricketer who was to be substitute in the English team for the man who is ill.'

And a 21-year-old draughtsman, who bought the *News Chronicle* from the station newsagent and read it in the train to and from work for 25 minutes in the morning and 40 minutes in the evening, was able at midnight to specify twelve political news items, eight items of light home news and one picture—with only a few mistakes. But by no means every one in this group reads his paper with such intensity. Some, for instance, like this young Londoner, hardly see the paper at all:

'I can't remember *which* papers I saw, for I didn't buy them, only glanced at other people's. In the early morning I pass a news stand at Hyde Park Corner and glance at all the papers displayed there, read the big headlines. Then at 9.30 the man who works in the same room with me comes in, and I look at his paper and I don't know which it is, but it's usually only when I know that there is something in it which interests me, like flying saucers recently. Today I didn't see his paper. Then at 7.30 if I go to dinner alone I sometimes buy a paper—any paper—to read while I eat. This wasn't the case tonight, but I read bits over a man's shoulder in a bus. I can remember three news items; there has been a further case of food poisoning, thought to be from tinned vegetables, and the Ministry are taking action. Mr Sartre is in London for the opening of his two plays in Hammersmith. He defines his philosophy in six words; he drinks double whiskies. And there is a new car on the market that will cost just over £1,000. It looks very nice and low, a sort of MG, I think. There was a photo.'

Analysis in general terms showed that of all the daily paper items actually remembered by this group:

> 38 per cent were political news items
> 30 per cent were items of home news
> 17 per cent were feature items (including 'gossip')
> 11 per cent concerned sport
> 2 per cent were comics and cartoons
> 2 per cent were advertisements.

It must be emphasized that remembering an item twelve hours after reading it is a very different thing to glancing at the headlines on first opening the newspaper. And yet, in general, two-thirds of all items recalled were news items against one in five features and one in ten sport.

The degree of news interest suggested by these results is particularly striking when it is compared to the amount of space given by the dailies to news. According to an analysis by *World's Press News*, in June 1947, the *News Chronicle* devotes 34 per cent of its editorial space to news, a higher proportion than any other daily paper. At the opposite end of the scale, less than a quarter of *Daily Mirror* space consists of news items, and in *The Times* the proportion is not much higher. *Roughly one-third of the papers read by our Panel group is devoted to news: yet two-thirds of the items that make the biggest impression on them are news items.*

This material shows clearly that although the more serious parts of the morning paper seem to be read sketchily and without much interest by a high proportion of 'ordinary' people, this proportion dwindles considerably when the group under observation is above-average in education and intelligence. The latter not only often read the paper thoroughly, the 'heavy' news items as well as the light, but also their average ability to recall what they have read many hours later shows that their reading is done with thought and interest.

Sunday Papers

To the Sunday reader, on the other hand, news is less important and features have a proportionately increased draw, a conclusion that is suggested over and over again by the material of this survey. *But even on Sundays more than half the items remembered by our Panel group at the end of the day were news items.* Table 6 compares results for dailies and Sundays:

TABLE 6

Percentage of all items recalled by Panel members at the end of the day, from their morning and Sunday reading, which fall into these categories:

Category	Morning Papers %	Sunday Papers %
Political news	38	30
Home news	30	26
Features	17	30
Sports	11	7
Comics and cartoons (including comic articles)	2	6
Advertisements	2	1

But although *numerically* news items are still remembered most of all, the *impression* they make on Sunday paper readers is much slighter than that made by features:

'I read the film, theatre, book and radio reviews. Can recall the criticism of Emlyn Williams' play, successful but not masterly, the story about the Welsh medium (fake) who has a success which kills him. Noted that Francoise Rosay's part was not considered good enough for her. No outstanding films, but re-issue of "Nanook of the North". Radio column in the *Observer* considered the delivery of talks by too-clever sounding experts. Could not complete the Crossword. In the news column noted Bevin's and Shinwell's speeches to miners at Morpeth with reference to "money-lenders" that seemed daring. Skipped Indonesian war, read political commentaries, but remember nothing. No outstanding books reviewed but read these columns as essays rather than for books to buy. Sports page for cricket scores. Remember nothing.' (*25-year-old Dublin doctor.*)

Probably one reason why Sunday interest in features is so much stronger than interest in news is that on Sundays so much newspaper reading is done casually, not only at all sorts of odd times of the day, but also with a feeling of relaxation rather than of duty:

'The newspapers were pushed through the front door, I tucked them under my arm and took my dog for her early airing in the fields. Then I skimmed the headlines of each as I walked slowly home. At breakfast I took the *Sunday Times* and my husband had the *Observer* and *Sunday Express*. I read Ernest Newman on Mahler and the book notice and an article on Gliding. Then I skimmed the *Sunday Express*, never taken seriously, and went on to the *Observer*, read Lejeune, Radio Notes and Nature Notes. Later, in the afternoon, I read all the papers right through.' (*31-year-old housewife.*)

Even amongst this middle-class group, features are the big Sunday draw. Later it will be seen that street sample material supports this conclusion, *and also that even where fresh news does attract the Sunday reader it as often as not takes the form of gossip and scandal.*

V: INSIDE THE PAPER

UNDER public library conditions people pay most attention to the news, and outside public libraries the same holds true of the more intelligent readers who submitted to the test described in the last chapter. But does this apply also to the average person, reading the paper in his own home?

To find this out, readers of every sort of paper were asked, 'What are the main things you like about it?' In addition a deeper probe was made into morning paper habits and attitudes, with questions on dislikes as well as 'likes', and also questions designed to discover which parts of the paper were read and which were never read.

Except among readers of the *Daily Mirror* and the *Daily Graphic*, news is always the main thing liked; and even amongst readers of these two picture papers more than half say that they read the news. On the other hand, this is by no means always 'serious' news. The following table compares Sunday papers, dailies, evenings and local weeklies:

TABLE 7

Percentage of people reading a Sunday, daily, local weekly and evening paper who say this is the main section of it that they like:

Section	Daily %	Sunday %	Evening %	Local Weekly %
News	27	21	38	47
Gossip, scandal	2	15	22	9
Sport	12	13	13	6
Comics, cartoons	10	2	3	—
Feature articles	10	24	6	4
Editorial	10	4	2	1
Letters	9	3	2	2
Political line	8	3	7	—
Pictures	6	7	9	2
Cinema announcements, etc.	—	—	—	6
Advertisements	—	—	—	24
Vague—generally approving	22	14	15	2
Miscellaneous	5	14	9	2
Don't know	5	9	10	10

(*N.B.*—Percentages add to more than 100 as many people give more than one reply.)

[1] Categories used in analysis inevitably involved a certain number of arbitrarily made distinctions. Rough working definitions, as they were assumed in analysis, may help to clarify the situation (*note continued overleaf*).

Nearly half the readers of local weeklies say that the main thing they like about the paper is the news; but in most cases this is local news. After local papers, it is readers of evening papers who mention news most; but here again it is significant that 'gossip and scandal' are mentioned by one person in every four or five, an indication that when 'news' alone is mentioned gossip is often meant as well as serious news. Sunday papers also are frequently enjoyed for their gossip content and least of all for more serious news. *It is only in the case of morning papers, more than a quarter of whose readers say they like the 'news', that gossip and scandal are seldom mentioned.* Again it is significant that morning paper readers most often mention the editorial, with readers of Sunday papers in second place; evening and local paper readers hardly mention the editorial at all. Letters and comics also arouse most interest amongst readers of morning papers. Feature articles (including reviews) are mentioned by one Sunday paper reader in four, but are considerably less important in every other sort of paper; and the 'miscellaneous' category (which includes serial stories, crosswords, recipes, and other features not subject to classification as articles), also occurs most amongst readers of Sunday and evening papers.

It is an interesting indication of the relative strength of interest in the feature content of Sunday papers, that Sunday readers mention the political line of the paper considerably less than readers of daily papers, morning and evening; later it will be seen that Sunday papers are chosen less for their political outlook than either

---

A. News: All news reports, excluding sport and the more gossipy type of personal news.

B. Gossip and scandal: personal news with a purely gossip interest (*Star* Man's Diary, divorces, film stars' private lives, etc.).

C. Sport: Sports news, comment, results, both on and off the regular sports page.

D. Comics, cartoons: Strips—comic and semi-serious cartoons.

E. Feature articles: Any form of feature material that could be said, broadly speaking, to take article form (excluding, for instance, serial stories, crosswords).

F. Editorial: Editional *comment* on the news.

G. Letters: Letters to the Editor.

H. Political line: included any mention of the paper's political leanings.

I. General: mention of layout, presentation, lack of bias, sensationalism, vague comments, etc.

J. Misc.: this consisted *mainly* of features which were excluded from the section 'feature articles'—crosswords, serial stories, texts, radio programmes, etc.

morning and evening dailies. Readers of local papers scarcely mention politics at all—in favourable context at all events; instead they are much more interested in the advertisements and local announcements. One in four mention advertisements as something they like about the local paper, and one in about sixteen mention announcements of cinema, theatre, meetings, etc.

General and vague replies occur most often amongst readers of morning papers: for the most part they consist of generalized approval, or favourable comment on layout, size, absence of bias, etc., e.g.:

'I like the whole of it.' (*Unskilled worker, 27, chassis erector.*)

'I don't know, I just look at it—I don't have much time, I'm at work all day.' (*Housewife, 35, artisan-class.*)

'It's not sensational, I always believe in it, there's no nonsense about it, it's always so dependable.' (*Housewife, 55, middle-class.*)

Asking people what they like about their paper is only one way of finding out the relative popularity of different parts of the paper. To provide a check on information obtained in this way, as well as to get a more all-round picture of the situation, readers of morning papers were also asked certain supplementary questions covering:

    (*a*) which parts they disliked,

    (*b*) which parts they read first, second, and subsequently

    (*c*) which parts, if any, they never read.

The table on the next page summarizes the results.

The relation between *liking* and *reading* provides an interesting key to interest and attitude. Twice as many people say they read the editorial, as mention liking it, and in the case of the news the difference is even bigger. Sport and cartoons both show a similar ratio of two *reading* to every one *liking*. Letters and feature articles, on the other hand, are spontaneously mentioned as 'liked' nearly as often as they are 'read', whilst pictures show almost no difference; each of these three kinds of features are quite clearly read with more enjoyment than either news, editorials or sport. For instance, there is the case of a 25-year-old housewife, who said that the first thing she read in the *Daily Mirror* was the news; asked what she *liked* about the paper she replied:

TABLE 8

Percentage of people reading morning papers who say that this is what they like, dislike, read, or never read in the paper[1]

	Like %	Dislike %	Items Read %	Never Read %
News	27	—	73	2
Gossip	2	1	4	1
Sport	12	2	27	26
Comics, cartoon	10	3	19	4
Feature articles	10	—	15	5
Editorial	10	1	20	2
Letters	9	—	14	4
Political line	8	5	—	—
Pictures	6	1	7	—
Advertisement	—	—	2	6
Nothing	—	75	—	48
General	22	—	—	—
Miscellaneous	5	8	11	8
Don't know	5	4	2	2

(*N.B.*—Percentages add to more than 100 because many people mention more than one item.)

'I like the pictures, it has nice pictures, and I like Patsy.' (*Unskilled working-class woman, 25.*)

Compare this reply with the interest shown by another housewife in the *Daily Mirror's* features. This time the 'like' question is answered with not much more enthusiasm than the question on what is actually read:

'I like Noel Whitcombe, of course, and I love Jane. I go all out on Noel Whitcombe, I think he puts what he has to say ever so well.' (What do you generally read first?) 'Well, I start off with Live Letters—it gives you a lot of information. Then I generally read the cartoon, and go on to Noel Whitcombe, and I make a point of reading Viewpoint.' (*Housewife, 45, artisan-class.*)

It is interesting that only a quarter of all the morning paper readers interviewed say that there is anything that they dislike about their paper, and of these many mention only external factors such as size, layout, etc. One in twenty says that he dislikes his paper's politics—

[1] This was based on results of three questions, analysed together. Readers of morning papers were asked what they generally looked at first when they got the paper, and, if the answer was 'the news', what they looked at after that; thirdly, they were all asked if there was anything they generally looked at subsequently, and if so, what? Combination in analysis of answers to all questions means that these figures represent all the chief items remembered as looked at in the paper.

or one particular aspect of its political outlook; the 3 per cent who dislike the comics and cartoons are chiefly *Daily Mirror* readers, with a few *Daily Mail* and *Daily Express* readers as well.

But this apparently low level of unfavourable feeling is less an indication of satisfaction, than a general lack of criticism. *People do not, for the most part, read their paper with any degree of care or judgment and it is relatively seldom that they think about it sufficiently, or have sufficient interest, to be able to criticize.* Although few people go to such an extreme, many show something of the uncritical acceptance of the country woman who, asked if there was anything she disliked about the *Daily Express*, her 'favourite' paper, replied:

'No, it's a newspaper, that's all.' (*Unskilled working-class woman*, 35.)

In spite of this, nearly half the entire sample of morning paper readers say they read everything in the papers. But this figure should certainly not be taken literally as an estimate of the numbers actually reading the paper from end to end; standards of thoroughness vary immensely from person to person. A few would really appear to miss nothing:

'No, every page is turned over two or three times a day.' (*Housewife, artisan-class*, 41.)

'No, I read it all. If I don't get through it one day I read it the next.' (*Housewife, unskilled working-class*, 50.)

But more are suspiciously casual:

'I skip through all of it, I think.' (*Housewife*, 65, *unskilled working-class*.)

And a working man who said there was nothing he didn't read, had immediately before described his reading routine as:

'It all depends on the mood I'm in. Usually I read the Live Letters first. Then I look at the pictures or anything interesting.' (*Unskilled working man*, 55.)

This man thinks he has read the entire paper when he has looked through everything that has appealed to him, or struck him as interesting; from the casual wording and general absence of criticism it seems likely that most of the people who say they read through all the paper are in actual fact almost equally selective in their reading. People tend to forget the things in which they are not interested—such as

33

the advertisements, for instance, which 4 per cent mention reading, 6 per cent say they never read, and the remainder of the sample do not mention at all.

The chief thing people say they do not read is sport—mentioned by one in four as something in which they have no interest. Sport is a specialized subject bound to hold no interest for as many people as it attracts; women are particularly inclined to ignore it completely. But the sports page is the *only* part of the paper—except possibly the advertisements which quite clearly people take for granted even if they do not read them—consciously ignored by any large-sized group. Not more than 5 per cent mention never reading any other single part of the newspaper's contents.

On the whole this material supports the earlier indications that the morning paper reader appears to pay most attention to the news, and editorial comment on the news, even if it is not this that he most enjoys. Other parts of the paper—sport, feature, pictures, etc.—may be read less, but often with much more interest and real enjoyment. In Sunday papers, on the other hand, more attention is given to features, and less to news; even where the news is read on Sundays, as often as not it is just scandal and light gossip. Moreover, in every sort of paper, reading is for the most part sketchy, and is normally given little real care or thoughtfulness.

Group Differences

Finally, a brief summary of group differences, starting with the influence of *sex*. Men are rather more interested than women in news, and considerably more in editorials. They are more or less the only sporting enthusiasts since of the entire sample of morning paper readers only one woman mentioned enjoying sports news. Women, on the other hand, read letters or comics and look at pictures more than men, and more often mention the gossip in the local and evening papers. They are also vaguer and more inclined to say they concentrate on the lighter aspects of the paper. Opinion poll work shows more or less consistently that on all semi-intellectual matters women as a group tend to be less interested than men, and less inclined to have an opinion; it is only when the question involves a personal or emotional issue, or has a fairly direct personal application, that their interest becomes stronger.

Age differences are less pronounced. Older people are more interested in editorials, younger people in comics, and letters. The younger age-group mentions local sport more than older people, but interest in national sports news scarcely varies with age. Rise in *income* increases the tendency to read the news, editorials and feature articles, and people in the higher income groups tend to read the paper for its political line more than the less well-off: the latter spend more time, in Sunday papers at least, on pictures and gossip news.

Educational level increases the importance attached to the paper's politics, and also develops interest in the news, editorial, and feature articles. The less well-educated give more importance to news and gossip in the Sunday paper and more to sport. *Voting* differences reflect the same trend. More Conservatives and Liberals show interest in news, editorials and feature articles than either Labour sympathizers or those with no political attachments at all.

On the whole, it is clear that news, editorials and feature articles tend to group themselves together as more or less serious reading, generally more interesting to men, the higher income and education groups, and possibly also to older people.

The survey now turns from a discussion of papers in general to a study of each section of the paper individually. We have already in a previous chapter made some brief references to the known age, sex and class variations that exist among readers of individual national daily and Sunday papers, and we now concern ourselves with the various parts of the papers that people like to read and what it is they like about them.

VI: THE NEWS

'You know it is all reading, sort of thing, something to read. To see how things are going on in the world. I like to hear about murders, I hear about all the murders going on, how it all happened. Proper blood curdler for that sort of thing I am.' (*Woman, unskilled working-class,* Daily Mirror *reader.*)

THIS *Daily Mirror* reader sums up fairly accurately the way most people tend to feel about the news. At its best news is well spiced with crime and sensation; but in any case it is all 'something to read', and on that basis many will accept almost anything, more or less uncritically.

News Readers

This taste for sensation may help to explain why the average public library reader spends most of his time on the news and how it is that even amongst readers in the street sample 73 per cent say at least that they read the daily paper headlines, while as few as 2 per cent admit that they do not read the news at all.

In striking contrast only 27 per cent of all morning paper readers mention the news as something that they particularly like about the paper. As an estimate of interest in relatively *serious* news this last figure is certainly the more reliable one. Very roughly it seems likely that in the street sample results, the 27 per cent who say they like the news represent a maximum estimate of those who take in what they read with some degree of serious interest; on the other hand as many as 49 per cent read the news without mentioning it as a part of the paper that they like best—and this group probably just glances at the headlines, skims through the news casually, or selects the most entertaining parts. And at the very lowest level, least news-conscious of all, 17 per cent neither like nor read the news, gossip or editorial, and are uninterested in their paper's political line. It is this group which concentrates more or less exclusively on features alone, or reads the news only when it provides something outstandingly entertaining.

The really indifferent, and the really interested, where news is concerned, consist of minority groups, one at each end of a normal curve.

36

Not many people, for instance, are as indifferent to the news and the way it is presented as this country workman:

'I read the *Mirror*. Not anything particular I like about it at all, except the cartoons. I don't read any particular page, just if anyone says anything interesting I pick it up and read it, but I don't bother with it much.' (*Unskilled working-class man*, 45.)

Verbatim records of replies to these questions make it clear how vague even *professed* interest in the news can be. Even so, those people who spontaneously mention the news, however casually, are at least showing some sort of conscious awareness of the fact that newspapers contain news:

'I like the comic cartoon strips, and it gives a good average of the day's news.' (*Unskilled worker*, 30, Daily Mirror *reader*.)

'Well, I like the fact that I can get a summary of the news at a glance, and it doesn't have the vulgarity of the *Mirror*.' (*Middle-class man*, 30, Daily Graphic *reader*.)

'The news' is not always so vague a term. It has already been shown that two-thirds of all the items that members of Mass-Observation's Panel remembered at the end of the day were news items, particularly political news. And in the street sample, too, there are indications of interest specifically in serious news. One such sign is the coupling of the news with the leading article; another is the ability to comment on it critically:

'The news—and the fellow who writes the leader every day.' (*Sanitary Inspector*, 58, News Chronicle *reader*.)

'It seems fairly unprejudiced and it puts the news clearly without exaggeration in any particular form.' (*25-year-old woman, middle-class*, Daily Telegraph *reader*.)

And some go so far as to object to news which consists largely of gossip and scandal:

'There's not so much of that stuff splashed about; I imagine one gets the news less decorated. I hate reading about other people's dirty linen.' (*Middle-class woman*, 40, Daily Telegraph *reader*.)

But for the bulk of the people, falling between the two extremes, morning paper reading means a source of moderately light news reading, mixed with a supply of sports news, cartoons and 'funnies', features and gossip. Even so, however little importance people attach to news other than gossip, this report has clearly shown that the bulk of reading is in fact news reading. In particular it seems clear that the paper's *presentation* of the news plays an important part in determining choice of paper. This will be discussed in detail later, but analysis of critical general comments on morning papers, for instance, shows that roughly one person in every four or five makes some reference to the way in which the news is presented. One in every nine of the whole sample felt that their morning paper gave the news without political bias, whilst an additional but rather smaller proportion, said it was straightforward, or gave the 'truth', without specifically mentioning political bias or lack of bias. Thus the proportion who are sufficiently conscious of the news content of their paper to comment on its presentation is not much smaller than that which spontaneously mentions the news as one of the paper's attractions; it seems fair to take this as support for the conclusion that although not every one of those who would like to be regarded as 'news readers' really deserve the title, *there is a sizeable minority of between a quarter and a fifth of all readers, who read the news—particularly serious news—with real care and judgment, and who must be expected to use news presentation as a criterion in making their choice of paper.*

Individual Dailies

The following table shows how interest in the news is distributed amongst readers of the different morning papers:

TABLE 9

Percentage of readers of these Daily papers who say they read, or particularly like the news[1]:

Paper	Like the News %	Read the News %
Daily Telegraph	47	81
Daily Express	35	80
Daily Mail	26	83
Daily Herald	25	85
News Chronicle	21	89
Daily Mirror	17	53
Daily Graphic	15	57

(*N.B.—Times* readers were too few for statistical results, but show a high level of interest in the news.)

[1] Details of the samples on which these and all subsequent newspaper tables are based are given in Appendix I of this report. It should be borne in mind here, however, that the size of the samples was not sufficient to give accurate representation to the newspapers with smaller circulations. For this reason the report hardly ever refers to the *Daily Worker*, and also for this reason percentages for such newspapers as *The Times*, the *Sunday Times* and *Observer* should be treated throughout with some caution.

Readers of the 'class' dailies, *The Times* and *Daily Telegraph*, show the highest level of interest specifically in the news, and picture paper readers the lowest; in the middle come the four main popular papers. On the other hand, if people who say they like the paper for its politics are added to those who say they like it for its news,[1] the *News Chronicle* and the *Daily Herald* come higher in the list, but still not so high as the *Daily Telegraph*.

In contrast, the following table shows how big a proportion of its editorial space each National daily gave to news—political, home and international, *only excluding 'crime and sensation'* during one week early in 1947[2]:

TABLE 10

Percentage of total editorial space given by these Dailies to news:

Daily Paper	%
News Chronicle	34·12
Daily Worker	30·63
Daily Herald	29·9
Daily Express	28·99
Daily Telegraph	28·44
Daily Mail	28·25
The Times	27·14
Daily Graphic	24·65
Daily Mirror	23·92

Readers of the *Daily Mirror* and the *Daily Graphic* like the news the least, and their papers devote the smallest proportion of space to serious news. *News Chronicle* readers are given the biggest percentage of news, and they, more than the readers of any other daily, mention it as something they read. Excluding the *Daily Worker* (for which only inadequate figures are available in this survey) the *Daily Herald* comes in second place in both cases. Generally there is little difference between papers in either percentage of space devoted to news, or percentage of readers reading it. Such a close relation between the amount of news content provided, and the reader's desire, or lack

---

[1] A not entirely justifiable procedure, since some people mention both; on the other hand, others who just say they like their paper for its political angle are implying that they like to read its news.

[2] These figures are taken from *World's Press News* for June 5th, 1947.

39

of desire, for news, again indicates that these may be important factors in determining *choice* of daily paper.

In a street questionnaire conducted as part of this survey people were asked to rate their degree of interest in a number of subjects suggested to them, amongst them interest in politics and foreign affairs. In both cases readers of *The Times*, *Daily Telegraph* and *News Chronicle* emerged as most interested, with readers of the *Daily Mail*, *Daily Express* and *Daily Herald* following close behind; least interested of all were readers of the *Daily Graphic* and *Daily Mirror*. *Nearly all* The Times *readers said they were interested in politics, but only one* Daily Mirror *reader in three.*

TABLE II

Percentage of readers of these Daily papers who say they are interested in politics and foreign affairs:

Daily	Politics %	Foreign Affairs %
The Times	94	97
Daily Telegraph	79	90
News Chronicle	69	66
Daily Mail	62	61
Daily Express	60	57
Daily Herald	55	50
Daily Graphic	46	42
Daily Mirror	33	38

It is particularly interesting that although readers of the *Daily Herald* and *News Chronicle mention* politics more than readers of any other paper as something they like about their paper, they actually appear to be less *interested* in politics than readers of either *The Times* or *Daily Telegraph*; in the case of the *Daily Herald* particularly, it would seem that the politics that determine choice of paper must be interpreted in a very broad sense of habit, background and class, rather than of conscious and actual interest.

A similar result emerged when people were given a more objective test of news-interest, by being asked to say which Government was at present in power in Jugoslavia. Results showed the mixed influences of education and political awareness, but again the readers of *The Times* and *Daily Telegraph* appeared to be most interested, with *News*

Chronicle readers in third place, followed by the other popular papers and with the *Daily Mirror* a long way behind. Only one *Daily Mirror* reader in every six was able to give the correct reply.

TABLE 12

Percentage of people reading these Daily papers who can say correctly which Government is in power in Jugoslavia:

Daily	%
The Times	87
Daily Telegraph	52
News Chronicle	43
Daily Herald	36
Daily Mail	36
Daily Express	35
Daily Graphic	35
Daily Mirror	16

Finally, a comparison again of *what people want and what they get.* The following table shows how much of its space each National daily gives to three different kinds of news:

TABLE 13

Percentage of editorial space devoted by these Dailies to:

Daily	Parliamentary Reports %	International Political News %	General International News %
News Chronicle	14·31	5·72	2·39
The Times	12·15	6·16	2·97
Daily Telegraph	11·60	6·17	2·61
Daily Express	11·40	5·59	1·17
Daily Worker	10·00	7·92	1·30
Daily Mail	9·45	3·26	1·99
Daily Herald	9·23	5·47	1·21
Daily Graphic	7·39	2·59	2·39
Daily Mirror	5·82	1·71	2·13

Readers of *The Times, Daily Telegraph* and *News Chronicle* seem to be most interested in politics, and these papers, with the *Daily Worker* (for which only inadequate figures are available), give the highest proportion of space to political news. The *News Chronicle* is slightly out of order in that its readers appear consistently less interested than readers of *The Times* and *Daily Telegraph* in political

41

news; yet the *News Chronicle* allows proportionately more space to politics. The explanation is probably the fact that, as will be seen later, *The Times* and *Daily Telegraph* have a reputation for unbiased reportage and solid, factual presentation of serious news: this may lead the politically most interested to read these papers even though they give less importance to political news. Even so, there seems to be a case for both of these 'class' papers giving proportionately more space to political news. But, on the whole, the dailies seem to give the right amount of space to political news to fit in with their readers' desires; again this can possibly be taken as an indication that degree of political interest is an important factor in determining choice of daily paper.

Personal Appeal

It seems likely that much reader-interest in the news is based fundamentally on some relatively undefined personal bond between the news and the person reading it. This may be a source of weakness (from the circulation point of view) for national morning papers, since their news has to cover so wide a field that to consider it in its personal application is beyond the ability—or the desire—of many of the less well educated. In this respect the morning paper is at a disadvantage compared not only with the local weekly and evening papers—with their store of local gossip—but also with Sunday papers whose development of 'scandal' news may be the root cause of their uniquely even appeal to people of every social class. Morning papers, on the other hand, seem to be read by working-class people largely in so far as they manage to establish with the reader some sort of personal appeal.

The *Daily Mirror*, for instance, is successful in this through its habit of putting a personal slant on its reportage, through its 'jaunty' layout, its use of pictures and cartoons, and its emphasis on home rather than international and foreign news. *The Times* and the *Daily Telegraph*, on the other hand, have little direct appeal to working-class people and their readership is predominantly middle-class.

Similarly, the *Daily Graphic*, read chiefly by middle-class women, has only the personal appeal channel of pictures (particularly attractive to women as will be seen later) and politics (attractive to Conservative sympathizers and therefore to the middle-classes). It seems likely that a paper's political sympathies are, in fact, closely related to this 'personal appeal' element. Later it will be shown that politics appear to be the strongest single factor determining choice of paper, and often this factor works through a process of similarity of political or class outlook, leading to a feeling of group sympathy and identification on the part of the reader. An illustration of this process is the *Daily Herald*, which has a wide appeal to the working man as the paper of his own social class.

Interest in morning paper news tends to increase slightly with advance up the educational scale, whilst interest in the more gossipy news of Sunday, evening and local papers, on the other hand, drops in the higher income and educational groups. This in itself indicates fairly clearly that the secret of the *Daily Mirror* in attracting high proportions of working-class readers, whilst lacking the working-class reputation of the *Daily Herald*, lies partly at least in its development of the lighter sort of news which has a strong element of personal appeal. In much the same way the fact that women and younger people are less interested in 'serious' news than men and the older age-groups, explains some of the *Daily Mirror's* attraction to young people and women. (Women mention their enjoyment of newspaper gossip and scandal considerably more than men, and apart from this they are less interested in the news of every sort of newspaper, only excepting the local weekly, with its easy personal associations.)

News for Children

Finally, news reading amongst children (on which information was also collected); 'crime' news is one of the three big newspaper interests amongst children, second in popularity only to cartoons. 14 per cent of all the items mentioned by children between 10 and 16 (the average number of mentions per child was $3\frac{1}{2}$) concerned crime. *Murders are particularly popular:*

'The *Daily Mail*. I like the murders and cartoons. Sometimes I read the whole paper.' (*14-year-old boy*.)

'I read the things that have happened to people—like murders, or burglaries, or anything like that.' (13-*year-old girl, reads* Daily Mail, The People *and* News of the World.)

Accidents make a very poor second to crime:

'Murders, amusing cartoons, readers' letters, anything amusing, things like aeroplanes breaking records and such things as crashes. And *crime.*' (13-*year-old boy, reads* Yorkshire Evening Post *and* Sunday Dispatch.)

Children's interest in crime declines steeply with age; crime mentions are as many as one in five amongst the 12-year-olds, but by the age of sixteen, they have dropped to less than half this frequency. And amongst the older groups there is sometimes a sprinkling of interest in more serious news:

'I read the headlines. I read about Russia. Murders, plane crashes, Parliament.' (15-*year-old girl, reads* Daily Mirror, Sunday Dispatch, Sunday Graphic *and* News of the World.)

'I like to read mystery, and police court trials. And the *Daily Mail* has a column written by a man whose name is Ian Coster, he writes short reports and Parliamentary happenings.' (14-*year-old boy, reads* Daily Mirror, Daily Mail, News of the World *and* Sunday Pictorial.)

But on the whole in so far as children are interested in the news it is crime and murder news, and where world affairs and Parliament are mentioned there is often a feeling that this is merely to make a good impression; crime news, on the other hand, is undoubtedly of genuine interest to them.

Sunday News-Readers

News interest in Sunday papers needs separate discussion from that of dailies. *Sunday paper readers give rather more importance to news, but for the most part in its sense of gossip and scandal;* one Sunday reader in every five of the general sample mentions the news as one of the things he likes about his paper, *and one in every seven specifically mentions gossip and scandal.* Many of those who only say they like 'the news' are probably really camouflaging their taste for gossip; but many others are quite open about their predilection for the slander and the scandal.

'I've had the *News of the World* for years. I like to read all the crimes and sensational things, and the medical part too.' (*Unskilled working-class woman*, 35.)

'I like the slander, and the scandal.' (*Middle-class woman*, 22, News of the World *reader*.)

And sometimes the real interest shows through the attempt to camouflage:

'I read the *News of the World*. It seems to me to have all straightforward news in it, and we've been having it for years.' (*Artisan-class woman*, 50.)

'The *News of the World*. Well, I like to settle down and read it of a Sunday afternoon. There seems such a lot in that paper compared with some of the others.' (*Unskilled working-class woman*, 21.)

But scandal is not always necessary to achieve a certain measure of direct appeal:

'I like the *Sunday Express* because of the little stories and articles that are interesting in it. That was interesting, all about the Commander who was in the Navy, all about his boyhood until he got on, and that sort of thing. I like all those stories they have in it about people that are alive, they are real life.' (*Housewife, artisan-class*, 40.)

In the *Sunday* memory test given to Mass-Observation panel members, results supported the conclusion that news seeking is less important a part of Sunday, than of daily paper reading. Every sort of news, even sports news, was remembered less in Sunday papers than dailies, and instead features left a much bigger impression. But news items still accounted for over half of all the items recalled, and political news still played the biggest part. However, news interest tends to increase with education and—as was the case with dailies— at the bottom end of the scale there is a corresponding minority group more or less indifferent to the news content of their paper; the Sunday paper featuring of gossip and scandal, however, may make this group rather larger this time:

'I read *The People*. I like the fashions and all that.' (*Unskilled working-class woman*, 36.)

'The *Pictorial*. . . . I took it for its animal pictures. But I don't read much of the news.' (*Woman hospital porter*, 37.)

'The *Sunday Express*; I like all the dirt, and the Duke of Windsor's memoirs.' (*Woman civil servant*, 40, *middle-class*.)

45

Individual Sunday Papers

Table 14 shows how the Sunday papers compare with each other in their readers' interest in the news:

TABLE 14

Percentage of readers of these Sunday papers who say they like the news:

Sunday Paper	%
News of the World	26
Sunday Dispatch	22
Sunday Graphic	22
Observer	21
Sunday Express	18
The People	18
Sunday Pictorial	17
Sunday Times	13
Reynolds News	9

The confusion of serious news with gossip is quite apparent. Readers of the *News of the World* show more 'news' interest than readers of any other Sunday paper; in addition to this, however, two *News of the World* readers out of every five say they particularly like the gossip and scandal; apart from these and readers of *The People*, no other Sunday paper readership mentions gossip any more than the readers of daily papers.

One of the subjects in which we asked people to rate their degree of interest was crime. Least interested, according to their own estimates, were readers of the *Sunday Times, Observer, Reynolds News* and the *Sunday Graphic*. The Sunday search after gossip and scandal is quite clearly relatively slight in these four papers, but it is not necessarily replaced by interest in more serious news-reports.

Only 3 per cent of the Sunday paper readers, compared with 10 per cent of the readers of daily papers, mention their liking for the politics of their favourite paper; later it will be seen that in Sunday papers politics is a much slighter influence in determining choice than it is with dailies. But readers of *Reynolds News*[1] mention its political angle more often than the readers of any other Sunday paper, even the *Sunday Times* and *Observer*, and this seems a fairly sure indication of genuine news interest. *Other tests show that readers of* Reynolds News *and of the two class papers, closely followed by readers*

[1] See Table 44 in Appendix III.

46

of the Sunday Express, *are most interested in international and political news, and best informed about it.* Nearly all the readers of the *Sunday Times* or the *Observer*, for instance, and two-thirds of the readers of *Reynolds News* and the *Sunday Express*, claim to be interested not only in politics but also foreign affairs—against only two-fifths of the readers of the *News of the World*.

Even more significant is the result of asking Sunday paper readers which Government was in power in Jugoslavia:

TABLE 15

Percentage of people reading these Sunday papers who can say correctly which Government is in power in Jugoslavia:

Sunday Paper	%	Sunday Paper	%
Observer	71	Sunday Dispatch	36
Sunday Times	69	The People	32
Reynolds News	60	Sunday Pictorial	24
Sunday Express	44	News of the World	23
Sunday Graphic	42		

Fewer than a quarter of the readers of the *News of the World* and of the *Sunday Pictorial* pass this news-interest test, against at least three out of five of the readers of *Reynolds News* and the *Sunday Times* and *Observer*.

Naturally these results are not conclusive. However strong a person's interest in the news they may still ignore it in one paper if they find it elsewhere in a form that they prefer. In particular the *Observer* and *Sunday Times* may be read for their features rather than their news reports, especially since so many of their feature articles are written on political subjects. Later it will be seen that *Reynolds News*, on the other hand, has a poor record in so far as feature interest goes; but it seems likely that it may to a certain extent compensate for this by attracting some of those people whose interest in news and politics carries over even to Sundays.

On the whole it seems likely that *Reynolds News* and the *Sunday Times* are most read for their serious news (the first partly because of the high proportion liking it for its politics, the second largely because of its readers' strong degree of editorial interest). The *Observer*, on the other hand, is probably read even by politically-minded readers as much for its feature articles as specifically for its news reports.

47

VII: THE EDITORIAL

'We take the *Daily Telegraph*. . . . Well, it's a Conservative paper isn't it? It was the leading article we wanted.' (*Middle-class woman, 50.*)

Eᴅɪᴛᴏʀɪᴀʟ readers represent the peak of serious news interest, and it is in this sense particularly that they deserve a chapter on their own. One morning paper reader in every ten mentions the editorial as something that he likes about his paper—compared with less than one in twenty of Sunday readers, and one in fifty of the readers of evening and local weekly papers. On the other hand, as many as one-fifth of all morning paper readers say they actually *read* the editorial, a contrast which indicates that some people at least regard their editorial reading as a routine, comparatively unexciting affair.

Very few people say they dislike or never read the editorial, but this seems partly because lack of interest in news and editorial is characterized by apathy rather than dislike, and partly because people are unwilling to admit such lack of interest. As an indication of the number of people who do not read the editorial, the 2 per cent who actually say they never read it is of little value compared with the 80 per cent who just do not mention reading it. The remaining figure of 20 per cent is likely to be a reliable measure of moderately consistent interest in the editorial, although it must be remembered that there are many others who read the editorial either so irregularly, or with so slight an interest, that they just do not think to mention it.

Whether or not people read the editorial is largely decided by their class, sex and educational level, and the group that does read it, the 'serious-minded' minority, tends to regard it with the sort of stable approval that seldom rises to enthusiasm:

'I read the *Chronicle*. The literary style is top-flight, and the leaders are very fair—the quality has always struck me.' (*Retired bank official, 65.*)

'I read the *Herald*, because of the leading article. I think it's a proper working man's paper.' (*Unskilled working man, 70.*)

48

The following table shows how the different papers compare in the importance given by their readers to editorials:

TABLE 16

Percentage of people reading these daily papers who say they particularly like or read its editorial:

Daily Paper	Particularly Like Editorial	Read Editorial
	%	%
News Chronicle	17	29
Daily Mail	12	24
Daily Express	11	24
Daily Telegraph	10	37
Daily Graphic	9	9
Daily Herald	4	15
Daily Mirror	3	3

(*N.B.*—*Times* readers were too few for statistical results but *more than half* of them say they read the editorial.)

TABLE 17

Percentage of people reading these Sunday papers, who say they particularly like the editorials:

Sunday Paper	%
Sunday Times	22
The People	7
Sunday Express	5
Reynolds News	4
Observer	3
Sunday Pictorial	3
Sunday Dispatch	2
News of the World	1
Sunday Graphic	1

Differences between Sunday papers are only slight, except for the *Sunday Times* which as a 'class' paper shows a high level of editorial reading; *Observer* readers, on the other hand, give much less importance to the editorial, concentrating instead on the critics and reviews. Here, then, is an answer to the question in the last chapter of how far the relative absence of gossip-seeking in *Sunday Times*, *Observer*, *Reynolds News* and *Sunday Graphic* is replaced by interest in serious news reports. Table 17 suggests that (apart from *Reynolds News*, with its readers' tendency to say they like its politics) only

49

readers of the *Sunday Times* have any pronounced interest in serious news other than that contained in feature articles.

Working-class people mention editorials less than the higher-income groups, and it is the daily papers with the most working-class readership—the *Daily Mirror* and the *Daily Herald*—whose editorials are given least interested attention. After them comes the *Daily Graphic*, the other picture paper. Most editorial-minded are readers of the *Daily Telegraph* and *News Chronicle*. The ambiguous position of the *Daily Telegraph*, with its very wide discrepancy between numbers reading the editorial, and numbers particularly liking it, is possibly due to the class and educational character of its readership, to whom editorial reading is more than ever likely to become a matter of routine.

Editorials are read by men rather than women in the case of morning, evening and Sunday papers; local editorials are scarcely read by either sex. Age differences are not big, but there is a consistent tendency in every sort of paper for older people to read the editorials more than younger people. Similarly, reading of Sunday and morning editorials tends to increase with income and education; voting differences reflect the same trend, with most editorial reading occurring amongst Liberals and Conservatives.

On the whole, breakdown differences confirm what has already been suggested. Editorial reading, like interest in serious news, is a matter chiefly for men, older people, and the better-educated; it is for the most part also the concern of the same groups as those containing the highest proportions of people reading newspapers.

VIII: THE SPORTS PAGE

'The only thing my husband likes is the football results at the weekend.'
(*Stoker's wife, 28, reads the* London Evening News.)

Relatively few people are as *exclusively* interested in sport as the stoker husband of this London woman. Even so, the sports page is a special attraction for one in every eight of the readers of morning, Sunday and evening papers alike. Even more—as many as a quarter of all morning paper readers—say they *read* the sports news; only in the local weekly does sport plays a less important part in the paper.

But sports page enthusiasts are outnumbered by people who consciously ignore that part of the paper. Nearly twice as many say they do not read the sports page as mention not reading all the other parts of the paper put together. *It is clear that sports news, more than any other aspect of the papers' make-up, has a consistent and considerable group of non-readers.* It is also important to note that similar proportions read sport in the morning paper as never read it—in each case just over a quarter of all readers; the remaining half either read it less regularly, and with less interest, or else are so uninterested in it that they completely overlook its presence in the paper.

Verbatim replies illustrate this split in newspaper readership between the sporting enthusiast on the one hand, and, on the other, those who rather resent the importance given to sport. Some say the paper should contain more sporting news, others that it has too much already:

'I think as with most papers, it gives too much space to sport.' (*Unskilled working-class woman, 20, Daily Express reader.*)

'They've an awful lot of sport on the back page which I'm not interested in, but I suppose the men like it.' (*Woman, 35, artisan-class, Daily Mail reader.*)

Sporting interest varies considerably in degree. For a few people like the stoker mentioned at the beginning of this chapter, it is the only reason for buying the paper. And a young labourer gives the same impression:

'I read the *Express*. . . . All the sport, see? I like it for the sports events . . . there is a sports page by Frank Butler, I think it is.' (*Unskilled working man*, 19.)

For others interest centres on sport, but does not exclude other topics:

'I read the *Express*. Because I'm very interested in sports, I always read the sports page first . . . then I turn back to the front page and read the news, and go through the paper. . . . On Sundays I read the *News of the World*. I can't say why I like it—except it's a good paper as far as sport's concerned. I've always had it.' (*Artisan*, 40.)

'I started taking the *Mirror* about twenty years ago. I used to be particularly fond of sport, and there used to be a lot of sport in it . . . I particularly like the Live Letter Box, and that back page of sport.' (*Handyman*, 55.)

Still included amongst those who are very interested in sport are some to whom sports content is only of second or third importance:

'The *News Chronicle*. I like it because it is an unbiased paper . . . well, I read the front page news first, then I turn to the leader . . . well, then I return to the front page and pick out the stuff that interests me, then probably I'll have a look at the sports page—see the football results and boxing and rugger matches.' (*Artisan*, 33.)

And, at the other extreme, those who never read the sport:

'Well, I don't ever look at the sports page, I never read that—but that's the first thing my husband looks at.' (*Middle-class woman*, 35, Express reader.)

Sport on Weekdays

The next table shows how interest in sport is distributed amongst the different daily papers:

TABLE 18

Percentage of people reading these dailies who say they read, or particularly like the sport:

Daily Paper	Particularly Like Sport %	Read Sport %
News Chronicle	22	39
Daily Express	20	34
Daily Herald	18	46
Daily Mail	12	32
Daily Graphic	6	6
Daily Mirror	2	14
Daily Telegraph	—	9

(*N.B.—Times* readers were too few for statistical results, but very few say either that they read or like sporting items.)

Readers of the four big non-picture papers are most interested in sport, readers of *The Times* and *Daily Telegraph* least interested, and in between come the two picture papers, *Daily Graphic* and *Daily Mirror*.

A similar result emerged when people were asked to rate their degree of interest in dog-racing, horse-racing and football pools. Differences between the three groups of readers (those of popular, picture and 'class' papers) are more consistent than differences within them, but on the whole *Daily Herald readers emerge the most interested in watching gambling sports.* Class influences are important in deciding which groups of readers are most interested in which sport; *Daily Mail* readers, for instance, are most interested in horses and *Daily Herald* readers in pools and dogs. *Daily Mirror* readers are more interested than *Daily Graphic* readers in dogs and football pools, whilst *Daily Graphic* readers show more interest in horse-racing.

A further question was asked in the same questionnaire on active participation in sport, and this reveals some marked changes of position. Thus, although *Times* readers are just as uninterested in taking part in sport as they are in watching it, readers of the *Daily Telegraph* graduate from the bottom to the top of the list when activity comes into the picture. *Daily Graphic* readers show a similarly stronger interest in active rather than passive participation in sport, while readers of the *Daily Mail* and *News Chronicle* show signs of a reverse trend; they feature most in the gambling sports.

It is interesting, finally, to compare these interests with what they are given to feed on. A 1947 *World's Press News* analysis of amount of space given by each daily to sport showed the following result:

TABLE 19

Average percentage of total space given by each of these daily papers to sport:

Daily Paper	%
News Chronicle	15·4
Daily Graphic	15·2
Daily Mail	15·1
Daily Herald	15·1
Daily Express	12·12
Daily Worker	12·12
Daily Mirror	9·6
Daily Telegraph	5·8
The Times	4

Quality may be more important than quantity, and *Sporting Life* analysis of accuracy of race forecasts during six months of 1947 arranges the dailies in the following order:

TABLE 20

1. Daily Express
2. Daily Herald
3. News Chronicle
4. Daily Telegraph
5. Daily Mail
6. Daily Graphic
7. Daily Mirror

Daily Express readers as a group are above average in their interest in sport, but their chosen paper gives them a smaller proportion of sports news than the other popular dailies—although what it does supply (on racing at least) is apparently of the highest quality. Readers of *The Times* and *Daily Telegraph* are least interested in sport, and their papers put least emphasis on the subject. The amount of space given by the *Daily Graphic* to sport would seem to be out of all proportion to its readers' interests, especially since its racing forecasts do not appear to be as reliable as those of most other papers. The success of any attempt on the part of the *Daily Graphic* to build up for itself, along these lines, a more male and working-class readership would seem to be doubtful. To achieve this it would have to forfeit not only its political line but its picture specialization too, and would lose almost all its present individuality.

The Sunday Sports Page

Turning to Sunday papers, here, first of all, are differences between readers' *interest* in sport:

TABLE 21

Percentage of people reading these Sunday papers, who say they particularly like the sport:

Sunday Paper	%
Sunday Dispatch	20
News of the World	17
The People	14
Sunday Pictorial	12
Sunday Times	9
Sunday Express	8
Reynolds News	4
Observer	3
Sunday Graphic	—

Self-rating tests also reveal readers of the class Sundays as least interested in gambling sports, and suggests that the *News of the World*, *Sunday Pictorial* and *People* have the most consistently sports-conscious readerships. Readers of *Reynolds News*, according to their own estimate, follow close on these three, and actually head the list of football pool interest. *Sunday Express* readers appear fairly consistently as almost as little interested in sport as readers of the *Observer* and *Sunday Times*, while those of the *Sunday Dispatch* and *Sunday Graphic* waver according to the type of sport concerned. *On the whole readers of the* News of the World *emerge as most consistently interested in sport, and most likely to feel drawn towards the sports page.*

Who Reads Sport?

Group differences show that sport is almost entirely a male interest. Very few women say that this is what they like about any sort of paper; in the case of morning papers one man in every five says he likes the sport, but no women mention this at all; and nearly half of all the men in the sample mention *reading* the sports news in the morning paper, against only one woman in every twenty-five. At the opposite extreme one man in eight says he never reads the sport, in contrast to two women in every five.

Age differences are only slight, and also differences of income. Educational influences, on the other hand, show themselves in a slight tendency for interest in the sports page to decline with level of education, although sport in local papers seems to appeal fairly evenly to people of every educational level. On the whole sporting features and news do seem to have a similar appeal for men of every group, even though for women they consistently have very little interest. And lastly, they appeal to children. Questioning of schoolchildren on what they like to read in the paper shows that 14 per cent of all the items they mention fall into the category of sport. With crime news, sport comes second only to comics in the frequency of mentions among schoolchildren.

IX: CORRESPONDENCE COLUMNS

'When I answered the phone a voice bellowed at me "For goodness sake come and look at my bees". . . . "What's the matter?" I said. The voice replied, "If you could see my wife's face you'd know." ' (*Letter in* Sunday Express.)

'In a house near me lives a man with a family who has done no work since he came to live there. . . . Yet all day he is singing at the top of his voice "I'm so tired". What has he got to be tired of?' (*Letter from 'Reader' to* Daily Mirror.)

LETTERS *to the newspapers make popular reading largely in proportion to their frivolity.* Two papers, particularly, have exploited this development, the *Daily Mirror* and the *Sunday Express*—and, amongst readers of daily and Sunday papers respectively, each of these is supreme in its readers' interest in the correspondence columns.

Readers of these two papers find the letters light and amusing reading; only very few are irritated by them. A 25-year-old agricultural labourer, for instance:

'I don't like these Live Letters. I think some of the questions are silly, also the people who answer them are foolish.'

Generally a high proportion of readers succumb to the intimate personal appeal of these letter features, as well as to their liveliness and the ease with which they are read:

'I read the *Mirror*. I open it at the Live Letters—I read that when I'm feeding the baby.' (*Unskilled working-class woman*, 30.)

'I like what they call the Live Letter Box, that tells you home truths.' (*Man, cleaner*, 30.)

'I like Viewpoint. I always turn to it first, they tell you something about everything and everybody. Then I read Live Letters, I never miss them.' (*Housewife, unskilled working-class*, 50.)

'I read the *Sunday Express*. . . . I always read the letters—that's the first thing I always read—they have columns about tittle tats from all over the world.' (*Woman, artisan-class*, 19.)

Nearly a third of all readers of the *Daily Mirror* mention their fondness for the letters, compared with one in eight of all *Daily Graphic* readers, and not more than one in twenty-five of the readers of any other morning paper:

TABLE 22

Percentage of readers of these daily papers who say they read or particularly like the letters:

Daily Paper	Particularly Like Letters %	Read Letters %
Daily Mirror	29	36
Daily Graphic	12	6
Daily Herald	4	9
Daily Telegraph	3	14
News Chronicle	3	5
Daily Mail	1	2
Daily Express	1	3

(N.B.—*Times* readers were too few for statistical results, but although a number say they read the letters, few mention liking them.)

When people are asked which parts of the paper they *read*, however, the picture is not quite the same. The *Daily Mirror* still heads the list, with seven readers out of every twenty reading the letters, but this time the *Daily Graphic* comes fourth. One *Daily Herald* reader in eleven mentions the letters, but only one *Daily Graphic* reader in every seventeen, a drop which is difficult to explain. *But it is evident that the* Daily Mirror *readership is easily the most enthusiastically interested in letters, whilst readers of the* Daily Telegraph *are shown relatively often reading them without at the same time displaying the same degree of interest.* For some people the letters are one of the chief reasons for buying the *Daily Mirror*; it is doubtful whether this could be said of more than a very few of the readers of the *Daily Telegraph*.

Both 'Live Letters' and 'Viewpoint' in the *Daily Mirror* have been so successful in establishing their individuality that they are frequently referred to by name. It is incidentally an interesting sidelight on the relative popularity of the different papers that this feature naming habit has established itself amongst *Daily Mirror* readers particularly. For instance, although the *Daily Express* has a bigger readership than the *Daily Mirror*[1], *Daily Mirror* readers in our sample

[1] 1947 situation.

detailed *by name* three times as many features that they liked, and nearly five times as many features that they read as were mentioned by readers of the *Daily Express*. More than half of these specific mentions were of either Live Letter Box or Viewpoint. There seems little doubt that these two letter features have an individuality that must account for much of the popularity of the paper to which they belong.

In Sunday papers, letter reading is even more strictly confined to individual papers:

TABLE 23

Percentage of readers of these Sunday papers, who say they particularly like the letters:

Sunday Paper	%
Sunday Express	13
News of the World / Sunday Dispatch	2

(All others—less than ·5 per cent mentions.)

One in eight of all *Sunday Express* readers say they like the letters—and one in fifty of the readers of both *Sunday Dispatch* and *News of the World*; in no other paper does the percentage of enthusiastic letter readers amount to as much as half of one per cent.

Of daily paper readers, one woman in every five mentions reading letters, and one in six says that this is something that she particularly likes about her morning paper. Only one man in every twelve mentions reading the letters, and fewer still say they like them. Young people tend to take more interest in readers' letters than older people, but income and education make little difference. Amongst children they are not much read; letters form only 4 per cent of all the items mentioned by our sample of school children.

X: COMICS AND CARTOONS

'I read the *Mirror*. All I worry about is Buck. . . . I read the comic strips first, of course, and not much else. The strips are all I worry about unless I've got more time.' (*Unskilled working man*, 35.)

COMIC reading for many people is the high spot of the paper. Some, like the countryman quoted above, read the paper for nothing else; and for this *Daily Mail* reader, Rip Kirby is quite clearly a pleasure which she saves up for herself, but only with an effort:

'I start at the front and work right through, and although I like Rip Kirby I wait until I get to him.' (*Woman, artisan-class*, 35, Daily Mail *reader*.)

One person in every five claims that he looks at the comics and cartoon and the 'funny parts' of the morning paper, although only half as many mention them as something that they particularly like. On the other hand, even though only one in thirty say they dislike comics, this is more than mention disliking any other single part of the paper, even sport; and it is clear that there is a small minority that does not merely refrain from reading comics and cartoons, but goes so far as to resent their presence in the paper.

But, as might be expected, it is chiefly readers of the *Daily Mirror* who mention comics and cartoons. As early as 1942 a small Mass-Observation survey showed that seven people out of ten admitted to looking at newspaper strips at least occasionally, and of these a third were referring to *Daily Mirror* strips. And the present large-scale survey shows that one *Daily Mirror* reader in every four mentions liking the comics, and very nearly half say they read them:

TABLE 24

Percentage of people reading these dailies who say they read or particularly like comics and cartoons:

Daily Paper	Particularly Like Comics %	Read Comics %	
Daily Mirror	27	44	(N.B.—*Times*
Daily Express ⎫ Daily Mail ⎬	7	12	and *Daily* *Telegraph*
News Chronicle	4	7	contain no
Daily Graphic	3	26	comics or
Daily Herald	1	—	cartoons.)

59

A quarter of all *Daily Graphic* readers and a fifth of all *Daily Mail* readers say they read the cartoons, but not many of the readers of either of these papers say that these 'funny parts' are something that they particularly like about them. Once again it is clear that the *Daily Mirror* alone has attained any degree of individuality for their features of this type, and it is chiefly to *Daily Mirror* readers that comics and cartoons have a really emotional appeal.

Comic reading is almost entirely confined to the national morning papers with the solitary exception of the *Sunday Express*. 13 per cent of all *Sunday Express* readers, and 2 per cent and 1 per cent of the readers of the *Sunday Dispatch* and *Sunday Pictorial* respectively, mentioned comics as something they particularly liked in the paper. Not more than half of 1 per cent of the readers of any other Sunday paper mentioned them. The evening papers' comics play an equally negligible part, and to the reader of the local weekly they are completely unimportant.

Detailed analysis shows that in so far as *Sunday Express* comics and 'funnies' are mentioned by name, Nat Gubbins and Giles are by far the most popular. Beachcomber in the *Daily Express* is specified considerably less often than Nat Gubbins in the Sunday version. In the *Daily Mirror*, Jane is mentioned most often of all, with Buck Ryan a poor second; in third and fourth place come Belinda and Garth. Funny feature articles like Cassandra get only comparatively few individual mentions. On the whole the popularity of Nat Gubbins indicates that successful 'funnies' can take a verbal as well as a picture form, although it is doubtful whether this type of feature would be a success amongst a working-class feminine readership like that of the *Daily Mirror*.

Much of the popularity of the *Daily Mirror* strips may be due to their blending of reality and fantasy, and in such a way that people are easily stimulated into identifying themselves with the strip characters. Sometimes this identification becomes very apparent:

'I like Jane. I wanted to have a body like Garth's, but I've only got my own. . . . I think there could be more comics. . . .' (*Man, 35, artisan-class.*)

For a few people, on the other hand, newspaper strips are interesting to children only:

'Well, of course, there's pictures in it for kiddies, those comic strips, Pop-eye and that, that don't interest grown-ups.' (*Handyman, 55, Daily Mirror reader.*)

But on the whole the funny parts of the paper arouse enthusiasm in the people who like them, in contrast to those features whose *emotional* appeal is relatively insignificant—such as, for instance, the editorial. One way in which this emotional nature of the comic's appeal makes itself apparent is in the difference between the extent to which men and women say they enjoy them. A quarter of all women morning paper readers, for instance, say they read the comics and cartoons, against only a seventh of the men; twice as many women as men readers say they particularly like this part of the paper. But these women are, naturally enough, largely *Daily Mirror* readers and the sex difference in comic reading of evening and Sunday papers is negligible. The under thirty-fives also tend to read and like morning paper comics more than older people, again possibly partly a reflection of the *Daily Mirror's* abnormally young readership. Income and education seem to make little difference. In general it seems fairly clear that influence of sex and age alone have any significant effect on appreciation of comics and cartoons.

Lastly, comics are more popular than anything else amongst children. 18 per cent of all newspaper items mentioned by children are cartoons, strips and comics:

'I read about Jimpy, and the other one on the same page. And on Saturday in the *Daily Mirror* there is a special page for children.' (*13-year-old girl.*)

'I read the *Daily Mirror*, I like Garth, Jane and Buck Ryan. And the sports and the comic.' (*13-year-old girl.*)

'I read the headlines and things about the royal family, and sometimes comics. In the comic page of the *Daily Mirror* I read Buck Ryan, Belinda and Garth.' (*14-year-old girl.*)

On the whole, children, in these older age-groups at all events, seem to prefer adventure cartoons to more childish or more sophisticated ones. Rip Kirby is mentioned particularly often, but Jane, Belinda, Jimpy, Garth and Buck Ryan are all mentioned more than the specifically children's cartoons. It is clear that children must make up a big proportion of the readership of strips and cartoons, and although for the most part they share their interest with the adults of their family, it seems probable that the *Daily Mirror* is sometimes bought largely in recognition of its appeal to children. It is significant, for instance, that married people with children read comics and cartoons, as well as letters, more than any other group. And very occasionally the present survey has brought to light cases where the *Daily Mirror* is bought wholly for the sake of the children. A London policeman, for instance, who took the *Daily Mirror* as his only daily paper, explained to the interviewer:

'I prefer the *Chronicle*, but my little girl likes the *Mirror*.'

The whole question of children's share in choice of newspaper needs much further study, especially in so far as comics and cartoons are concerned. Our present investigation could attempt nothing more comprehensive than a pilot survey of this particular field.

XI: FEATURE ARTICLES

'I'm not interested in the paper from the news side, all papers contradict one another there. I always say don't take any notice of the news. Myself, I'm very fond of gardening—I always read Mr Middleton's column, it comes in useful.' (*Mechanic's wife, 45, reads* Daily Express.)

THIS London woman's exclusive concern with feature articles in her daily paper reading is an extreme case. On weekdays most people read the news at least sketchily, even though they may get more actual enjoyment from the features and feature articles. It is in the enthusiasm that they arouse, particularly, that interest in feature articles is strong; this is especially the case amongst Sunday paper readers, one in every four of whom mention feature articles as something that he particularly likes about the paper. Of readers of local weeklies, on the other hand, only one in twenty-five mentions feature articles, with one evening reader in seventeen, and one morning paper reader in ten. But the strong emotional appeal of this part of the paper for those who read it, even in the morning papers, is shown by the fact that *almost as many people say they like feature articles as mention them as something that they read.* In fact in the case of the *Daily Mail,* whose feature articles are most popular, more people spontaneously mention liking them than mention reading them!

Amongst daily papers, feature articles are most often mentioned by readers of *Daily Telegraph, Daily Mail, Daily Herald* and *News Chronicle*:

TABLE 25

Percentage of readers of these daily papers who say they particularly like the feature articles, or mention reading them:

Daily Paper	Read Feature Articles %	Like Feature Articles %	
Daily Mail	11	22	(*N.B.*—
Daily Telegraph	26	16	Readers of
News Chronicle	19	14	*The Times*
Daily Herald	20	14	were too few
Daily Express	15	9	for statistical
Daily Mirror	7	5	results.)
Daily Graphic	17	—	

Most popular features appear in the *Daily Mail*, but even here only one in every four or five is particularly drawn to features, compared with two-thirds of all *Observer* readers and more than half the readers of the *Sunday Times*:

TABLE 26

Percentage of readers of these Sunday papers who say they particularly like the feature articles:

Sunday Paper	%
Observer	69
Sunday Times	52
Sunday Express	40
Sunday Graphic	33
People	32
Sunday Pictorial	27
Sunday Dispatch	20
Reynolds News	17
News of the World	5

Readers of the *Sunday Times*, and of the *Observer*, mention feature articles particularly often largely because of the reviews in these papers. The 'Duke of Windsor' series running in the *Sunday Express* at the time of fieldwork on this survey caused much of the feature interest in that paper; and *Sunday Pictorial* readers mentioned the 'Birth of a Baby' feature almost exclusively. *Sunday Graphic* feature articles were seldom specified individually, except for occasional reference to the Rev. Elliot. Feature articles in *The People* consisted largely of Hannen Swaffer, Arthur Helliwell, Man of the People and Lyndoe. *Sunday Dispatch* readers were fewer, and feature articles correspondingly seldom specified by name; Joad got several mentions, but in any case the serial story (not classified amongst feature articles) was much more often mentioned. In the *News of the World*, where feature articles were not often mentioned anyway, only the Horoscope occurred with any frequency.

One of the most striking results emerging from this material is the fact that most of the Sunday papers are read for one single feature article, whereas feature popularity in the dailies tends to be spread over a much greater diversity of articles. Reviews in the *Observer* and *Sunday Times*, the Duke of Windsor (at that time) in the *Sunday Express*, and the 'Birth of a Baby' in the *Sunday Pictorial* are all specialized and *exclusive* items with a very concentrated appeal.[1] The *Sunday Dispatch* and *News of the World* have no single popular feature article, but make up for this lack, the one with its serial story, and the other with its exclusive and very popular gossip and scandal news. On the other hand, the papers whose readerships have increased little or not at all during the last five years are also the Sundays without any single outstanding features. It is possible that there is no relation between these two facts, but on the other hand, *it seems likely that striking individual features make up a large part of the Sunday papers' appeal, and lack of them may retard circulation increase.*

Here are some examples of people who read their Sunday paper for the sake of its main feature:

Sunday Times. 'I like reading the book and theatre reviews.' (*Housewife, middle-class*, 35.)

Observer. 'Its cultural background—the articles, films, paintings and things like that—I get it more for that than anything.' (*Middle-class man*, 24.)

Sunday Pictorial. 'How the baby's born and the pictures.' (*Woman*, 19, *unskilled working-class*.)

In daily papers, there is less concentration on single popular feature articles. In the *Daily Mail*, Don Iddon is most often mentioned, with Anne Temple and Frank Owen in second place. In the *Daily Telegraph* references are usually to 'Peterborough' or the woman's section, in so far as items are specified by name. *News Chronicle* feature articles show almost no *individual* concentration of appeal, even though feature articles *in general* are popular. In the *Daily Herald*, Hannen Swaffer and 'Woman Sense' stand out to a certain extent, but not strikingly; and the *Daily Express* has no outstanding feature article at all, in the sense that none is often mentioned by name. 'Cassandra' in the *Daily Mirror* is mentioned to a certain extent, but is completely overshadowed by mentions of the letters and cartoons. Lastly, Candidus in the *Daily Graphic* occurs

[1] There is no evidence to suggest that this concentration of interest on one single feature was in any way merely a chance development of the time during which this survey was carried out.

relatively often, with Kathleen Partridge in second place.

The conclusion that daily paper feature articles tend to have their popularity spread amongst a number rather than concentrating on a few accords with the indications, discovered elsewhere in this report, that in morning papers people expect an all-round coverage of news and features, rather than specific feature and magazine content. *It seems that varied feature content, not out of proportion to the amount of news space, is a draw in daily papers, whereas on Sundays it is an advantage to have one central feature with a strongly built-up individuality.*

Verbatims support this conclusion. When, for instance, people say they like a feature article in any daily paper (with the possible exception of the *Daily Mirror*), it is usually in conjunction with some other aspect of the paper.

'I think I like the "Woman Sense", and all the news bits they have of unusual happenings.' (*Woman, unskilled working-class,* 34, Daily Herald *reader.*)

'I read the *Express.* There seems to be a good assortment of everything in it, and I like the American news and the back page, and the crossword.' (*Woman, artisan-class,* 35.)

'The *News Chronicle.* I like its Liberal attitude—that is it gives both sides of the question without political emphasis or sensation. I like it on Saturday mornings—the film reviews, and Vicky's cartoons.' (*Middle-class man,* 24.)

Feature articles are mentioned more or less equally by men and women, but on the whole are given most importance by the higher income groups. Children, finally, mention them very little indeed.

XII: ILLUSTRATION

'The pictures are a help to you. You don't always want to read.' (*Housepainter's wife*, 65.)

PICTURES are simple and easy to understand, and it is in this facility that much of their attraction lies. The London housewife who says she does not always want to read is expressing the less conscious feelings of many others. Some people, for instance, buy the paper for its pictures alone:

'I like the pictures. I'd go a long way for a picture.' (*Cobbler, 50, reads the* Daily Mirror.)

Because of the simplicity of their appeal it is not surprising that women mention pictures more than twice as much as men, in Sunday papers as well as dailies. Other differences between groups are slight. Not many schoolchildren mention illustrative pictures, although there are many indications that interest may be strong amongst the very young children who are outside the scope of our investigation. Sometimes, for instance, the paper is bought largely for the sake of the small children of the family:

'I read the *Pictorial*. I buy it for the baby to look at the pictures.' (*Housewife, unskilled working-class, 30.*)

Roughly a fifteenth of all readers of Sunday and morning papers and very few local paper readers say that they like the pictures and photographs. They seem to appeal most of all to evening readers, one in eleven of whom say that this is one of the things they particularly like about their paper.

Naturally, it is the picture papers almost exclusively whose readers mention pictures and photographs (see Table 27 overleaf). Pictures are particularly important to one-third of all *Daily Graphic* readers, and to one-sixth of all readers of the *Daily Mirror*. For *Daily Graphic* readers this is the most popular sort of item only excepting

ILLUSTRATION

TABLE 27

Percentage of readers of these daily papers who say they look at, or particularly like, the pictures:

Daily Paper	Particularly Like Pictures %	Look at the Pictures %
Daily Graphic	32	34
Daily Mirror	18	18
Daily Mail	1	1
Daily Express	1	1
Daily Herald	—	2
News Chronicle	—	1
Daily Telegraph	—	—

(*N.B.—Times* readers were too few for statistical results but not many mention pictures.)

the news; in the *Daily Mirror*, on the other hand, pictures come only after the comics, the letters, and the news. It is here that one of the chief differences between the two 'picture' dailies becomes particularly clear. In both cases quick and lively presentation of the news is of highest importance to readers; but after this, *Daily Graphic* readers find pictures the chief outstanding feature of the paper; whilst readers of the *Daily Mirror* give second place in appreciation to its letters and comics.

The following table shows how high a proportion of their total editorial space each daily paper devotes to pictures:

TABLE 28

Percentage of total editorial space given by these dailies to pictures:

Daily Paper	%
Daily Graphic	17·66
Daily Mirror	12·88
Daily Mail	6·76
Daily Herald	4·86
Daily Express	4·41
News Chronicle	4·14
Daily Worker	2·50
The Times	1·90
Daily Telegraph	1·80

The close similarity between this table and the one above indicates not only that in so far as illustration is concerned each paper is giving its readers more or less what they want, but also that the different amounts of space devoted to pictures is one factor helping to determine choice of daily paper.

Amongst Sunday papers the difference between the pictorial and non-pictorial type of paper is even more striking. More than half of all *Sunday Graphic* readers, and just under half the readers of the *Sunday Pictorial*, say they particularly like the pictures. On the other hand not more than one reader in twenty-five of any other Sunday paper mentions pictures at all. It seems clear enough that in Sunday papers particularly choice of paper is to a considerable extent dependent upon whether or not people want to look at pictures. The impact of pictures is stronger than in daily paper reading where this factor, although important, is more deeply submerged amongst other considerations.

XIII: THE EVENING PAPER

Discussion of the way people feel about the inside of the paper has had, for clarity's sake, to leave out much of our available material on local and evening papers. The following chapter is a brief attempt to produce a more rounded and integrated picture both by recapitulation and by the filling-in of some of the gaps.

It has already been noted that news, serious and gossip matter together, is mentioned more in reference to evening papers than to mornings, Sundays or local weeklies. More than half the readers of both evening and local papers mention either news or gossip—but the sort of 'news' that most people are thinking of in local papers and evenings is very different to morning paper news. Gossip content is particularly important, as well as local news. A north country shop assistant, for instance, said that she read the evening paper because:

'I like to read all about the Borough, the little pieces of gossip and that. I like to read the cartoons as well, Lee and the Flop family. The miscellaneous sales, and the births, deaths and marriages. If I miss it one night I read it the next. I usually see it every evening at the shop before I go home.' (*Shop assistant, woman, 25.*)

And another woman in the same town:

'We like the local news—whatever happens you see it in the paper. I like the ——, we all like to see it when it comes; whatever happens, a fight or anything, it's always in. The woman serving in the grocer's shop threw three tins of peas at a customer because she was rude to her; I was waiting to see what would happen to her, it's in the paper today, she was fined £5. It's things like that I like to read about.' (*Unskilled working-class woman, 35.*)

whilst a Midlands woman keeps up with the news:

'I always look at the "situations vacant", and see if there's anybody I know that's died.' (*Unskilled working-class house-wife, 27.*)

But for some people the absence of features or anything but light, local news in the evening paper is a reason for not reading it. This man, for instance, reads the *Daily Mirror* for its features:

'When I've the time, I look at the *Mirror*—Live Letters—they seem to learn you a bit, they give you the answers, you know. And Jane! I've not much time to read really, but when I do I prefer the *Mirror*.' (*Unskilled working man*, 35.)

Given more features in the evening paper he might be less apathetic about it:

'I look through it, there's nothing in it—no news that's anything. Same as the *Echo*—nothing in it. The shipping is all I look for.'

Only 6 per cent of our sample mentions enjoying the feature articles in the evening paper, and as few as 3 per cent its comics and cartoons. This, however, is quite likely to be as much a reflection of what people are given as an indication of what they want. But even as the position is at the moment, features are sometimes the first thing mentioned in comments on the evening paper:

'It's a good paper—and the cartoon's one of the best of the day. Although Low's cartoons haven't been quite so good lately.' (*Small shopkeeper*, 45, *reads London* Evening Standard.)

A high proportion of evening paper readers are interested in the sports page; as many as one in seven or eight mention it spontaneously, and it is often bought for sports results alone.

'The news is more or less the same in all papers—when you've read one you've read the lot. But as I like a bet now and then, and the *Star's* a good sporting paper—that's what I read. It's very good for all sport.' (*Skilled factory worker*, 45, *reads London* Star.)

'I like the ——— for the racing results—to see whether I've won or not. I like to read the advertisements and that, and the miscellaneous sales. The news value doesn't bother me much.' (*Woman*, 45, *unskilled working-class*.)

Size, layout, and general presentation are particularly important to the evening reader:

'I like the print of it, and it's a nice sized paper.' (*Handyman*, 55, *reads London* Evening News.)

Sometimes the evening paper is read more thoroughly than the morning paper:

'The *Star* and *Standard* are both small papers, more convenient to read than the *Evening News*, I like doing the crosswords when I've time—but I generally spend more time reading an evening paper than the morning.' (*Artisan-class woman*, 45.)

And a north country newsagent comments:

'The morning papers aren't read so well as the evening papers. The men haven't got the time, they have to leave the house to get to work by eight o'clock and maybe they just have time to glance at the paper, the headlines,

71

and that's all. And the women haven't got the time either, not round here they haven't, they've got housework and shopping and queueing, and some of them work, too. But when they come home at night they like to sit down after a bit of supper and read the evening paper.

'The — *Evening News* is very popular, I sell more *Evening News* than all the rest put together. I've heard some of them grumble about it, they say it's a rag, but I notice they spend a lot of time reading it. They must do, because I've heard them talk about some little bit of local news that they couldn't have heard about if they hadn't read it in the *News*. Some people tell me they like to read all the ads in it. A lot of them are about local affairs and they find them interesting. They even read the "Situations Vacant". It's a funny thing about that, even if a man has a job and doesn't want a change he likes to see what kinds of jobs are going. . . .' (*Newsagent, working-class district.*)

But finally, one big disadvantage suffered by the evening paper is its Conservatism. Many people object to this—although they may still buy the paper for lack of choice:

'It's a Kemsley paper—I think it an insult to the intelligence of the Tees-side people, especially their leading articles—nine out of ten times it's just tripe. If an intelligent man writes that he certainly doesn't write an intelligent article. . . . I buy it because there isn't another paper in the area, no other evening paper at all.' (*Working man, unskilled, 45.*)

But this disadvantage would be much bigger if serious and political news were of more importance to the evening reader. On the whole it is light news and gossip that chiefly interests him, and only the more critical reader objects to political and technical in-adequacies in the evening paper. Even in Mass-Observation Panel, where criticism of the provincial evening paper on political and technical grounds is very common, many continue to buy it for its other advantages:

'The — *Evening Argus* is one of the poorest local rags I have seen. Its typography is poor, layout worse, its news content negligible, and its comment is, besides being naturally parochial, an echo of pre-war days. It is nevertheless the best advertising medium in the district, and is useful as an entertainment guide. I buy it if I am interested in either of these features.' (*Young man, Panel Member.*)

'Our sole local paper, the — *Evening Sentinel*, is one of these multiple mouthpieces of the Northcliffe group, it just stands for everything I dislike. Its standard of journalism is of the lowest with the exception of one writer, the music and drama critic. At one time I refused to read this paper, or to buy it, however, we find it necessary to give us the dates of concerts and, occasionally, films.' (*Young man, Panel Member.*)

XIV: THE LOCAL WEEKLY

'I can't be bothered to read local papers. Scandal-mongers, that's what they are, the people that read them—they're just trying to see what their neighbours have been doing. It's just a lot of scandal.' (*Cafe proprietor*, 55.)

THIS man, if he can be taken at his face value, is reversing the usual attitude; the gossip and scandal that he dislikes in the local paper are most people's reason for buying it. News with a strong flavour of gossip and local colour is for many people simpler to understand, as well as having a stronger personal draw. In her comment on the local paper, for instance, this London housewife makes her attitude to the national paper equally clear:

'I only read the local paper; there's a lot to do with local things, and I understand *them*, and the ups and downs of the rates which concern us.' (*Housewife, artisan-class*, 50.)

A charwoman, asked why she reads the local paper, makes her attitude quite plain:

"Lord love a duck! What a lot of silly questions. Just for curiosity of course. Not for anything in particular.' (*Charwoman*, 45.)

And another working-class reader of a north London local paper enjoys his sense of identification with local celebrities:

'Well, there's the general news of the village, local news—I read all about the famous Spurs.' (*Unskilled working-class man*, 78.)

Even so, there is no doubt that working-class people are more interested than the middle-classes in the local weekly. This is for the most part a matter of strength of feeling rather than of numbers approving and disapproving; but it is interesting that the local weekly is read equally by people of every income group, in spite of the more usual tendency for the better off to read more[1]. This is undoubtedly due to the attraction of gossip and local news; 'serious' news is of

---

[1] Only Sunday papers, with their strong element of gossip news, are read *more* by members of the lower income groups.

less interest to working-class people than to the more adequately educated middle-classes.

A supplementary question in the second part of our main survey asked local weekly readers how they felt about their paper. More than half those who replied did so more or less favourably, and only about a sixth disliked it without the qualification that they read it for its local news and gossip. The most striking thing about the replies, however, was the class difference. A much higher proportion of working- than of middle-class people are favourably disposed towards the local weekly, although middle-class people tend to make up for their lack of approval by indifference, or with a grudging admission that they read it, rather than by any outright condemnation. But to some extent it seems likely that the middle-classes are merely expressing what the less articulate working-classes feel. *In all groups favourable feeling is seldom enthusiastic and it seems clear that indifference is a very common attitude where the local weekly is concerned.* One in six expressing explicitly unfavourable feelings is probably a minimum estimate, based on the replies of those people who are most conscious of their feelings and most willing, and able, to express them directly.

At the lower level of the educational scale the local weekly is enjoyed because of the ease with which local events can be understood and absorbed, and because the reader is more likely to be concerned with a restricted circle of interests. The upper level, on the other hand, can to some extent be represented by members of Mass-Observation's National Panel of Voluntary Observers. In 1947, these were asked for an account of their habits and attitudes concerning the local papers of their area. Since the general term 'local paper' was used, many of the replies discussed provincial evening papers rather than local weeklies. As these present such a similar picture, however, they were all included in analysis of results, only excluding the London evening papers and any others with a circulation sufficiently widespread to forfeit their strictly local character.

The results are interesting. Two-thirds of the whole sample said they read local papers, the same proportion as reads evening papers in the general population, and rather more than reads local weeklies. One of the chief reasons why people in this group avoided the local paper was, again, its Conservatism. By no means representing an uncommon attitude is the remark of this woman member of Mass-Observation Panel:

'I don't buy any local paper. Most of them, I feel, are smug, and crawl cosily round their more Conservative readers.' (*Middle-aged country woman.*)

But those who read the local paper do so largely for its value as a source of local information and entertainment news:

TABLE 29

Percentage of Mass Observation Panel sample mentioning these items as something that they particularly look for in the local paper:

	%
Local items and events	20
Entertainment guide, reviews	20
Classified advertisements	18
Local politics	10
Letters	8
Births, marriages and deaths	8
Editorials	4
National News	3
Sport	2
Features	3
All items	4

Entertainment announcements and advertisements are each nearly as often mentioned as all the varieties of news; and of the latter *National news* forms only an insignificant part, about a tenth of the total news mentioned. Where there is more than one paper available the one with the most 'local colour' is generally chosen—although in some cases all are taken for various reasons, one for its advertisements, another for its relative lack of political bias, and so on.

In this middle-class group, opinion about local papers is almost equally divided between praise and criticism. But this does not mean that these people are equally favourable and unfavourable towards the local paper, since there is still one-third who, for one reason or another, do not read a local paper at all. Praise is given specifically for the local paper as:

TABLE 30

Percentage of total FAVOURABLE *mentions:*	%
1. A quick guide to local entertainments	23
2. A means of keeping in touch with local affairs	21
3. Its classified advertisements	18
4. A source of general information about the district	16
5. Political fairness	13
6. Opportunity afforded for expression of opinion on local matters	9

Whilst criticism is given for:

TABLE 31

Percentage of total UNFAVOURABLE *mentions:*	%
1. Political bias	43
2. Low standard of journalism and production	38
3. Syndicate ownership	13
4. Poor film reviews	6

Finally, the opinion of the majority of Panel members is well expressed by this young north country woman, in her account of her attempt to find a local paper that supplied more or less what she was looking for:

'When we came to live here, two months ago, we sought out a local paper in order that we might have information about concerts, films, lectures, etc., in the area. Our first trial was the local evening paper, but since this was a Kemsley Press do, we found little local news and almost nothing that would introduce us to whatever cultural world the town possessed. The bulk of the "news" provided dealt with London suicides and shady cases. Our next attempt was with the weekly paper, but this again was useless to us—again Kemsley popular stuff. . . . Discouraged we sought the — *Times*. Here at last we found an approximation of what we wanted, though the area covered was not strictly ours. But at least there was some intimation of how life was being lived in the surrounding villages, and more or less accurate reporting of meetings held by councils, clubs and committees. So we continue to buy it, and look to it to provide us with advertisements of local rather than national interest, reports of local events, and intimations as to which way the wind is blowing in the communities which surround us. If we want the sort of stuff the Kemsley Press offers, we can get it from the dailies, but we certainly don't want it as a substitute for local news; in these days of decreasing individuality one doesn't want too much of "the world is my parish" idea. Rather let us have local news as it stands, even though it seems to lack the

76

pep of the more spicy news from London and other centres of vice and excitement.'

This is the attitude of most of the middle-class Panel and, *in its more positive aspect* it is typical of much of what is felt by the ordinary person. Most people are less conscious than this of what they look for in the local paper, and are certainly neither so deliberate in their choice nor so aware of the local paper's politics. And many, as has been seen, are completely uncritical because the local news supplies all their wants, both intellectual and emotional, and there is no comparison or overlapping with the national paper. But for the most part, the local paper is quite clearly enjoyed for its local information alone.

XV: THE NEWSPAPER'S IMPACT

In many ways the most important topic concerned with newspaper reading is the question of how far people are influenced by what they read. Even before making this survey, in the course of which several attempts were made specifically to throw light on this problem of Press impact, Mass-Observation files had accumulated a certain amount of information on the subject. In all, the following aspects of the influence of newspapers have been explored:

(a) Editorial influence on opinion.

(b) The impact of reviews, specifically on cinema-going.

(c) The impact of the sports page, specifically on filling in football-pool coupons.

(d) The influence of the Press in relation to that of other opinion-forming media—e.g. books, radio, etc.

Editorial Influence on Opinion

During the 1947 Gravesend by-election, a sample of 500 people were tested for their knowledge of the candidates, and the results correlated with their daily newspaper reading. Rather more than half the sample was able to give the name of both candidates; just under a quarter could name neither. Table 32 breaks this result down by daily papers:

TABLE 32

Percentage of readers of these daily papers able to give the name of these by-election candidates[1]:

Candidates named	Daily Telegraph %	Daily Express %	News Chronicle %	Daily Mail %	Daily Herald %	Daily Mirror %	TOTAL %
Both	79	68	64	60	56	41	57
Labour only	5	6	14	8	10	15	11
Conservative only	3	9	10	17	10	11	10
Neither	13	17	12	15	24	33	22

[1] As this is a relatively small-scale survey, results for the smaller-circulation dailies, must be interpreted with caution; for this reason, too, figures for *The Times* and *Daily Graphic* have been completely excluded.

Rearranging this table to show how the papers compare in respect of *their readers' inability to name either candidate*, the following picture appears:

TABLE 33

Percentage of readers of these dailies who cannot give the name of either by-election candidates:

Daily Paper	%
Daily Mirror	33
Daily Herald	24
Daily Express	17
Daily Mail	15
Daily Telegraph	13
News Chronicle	12

Daily Mirror readers remained most unaware of the election campaign, with as many as one-third unable to name either candidate. The other very working-class daily, the *Daily Herald*, came next in unawareness, with one reader in four unable to give any names; the *Daily Herald* readership is predominantly male, and strongly Trade Unionist, whilst the *Daily Mirror* readership is equally divided between the sexes; this difference may operate towards a lesser susceptibility to election propaganda on the part of *Daily Mirror* readers, and there is also the probability that the *Daily Mirror* gave less prominence to the election than the *Daily Herald*.

A more useful indication of the impact of the paper is provided by another part of the same by-election material. An investigation into the newspaper composition of the 'floating vote' suggested that of the middle and left-wing dailies the *Daily Herald* and *News Chronicle* had a higher proportion of readers changed over from Liberal and Labour to Conservative than the *Daily Mirror*; on the other hand the *Daily Herald* also showed the strongest tendency towards switch-overs in the reverse direction. Probably it is the relative lack of political interest existing amongst *Daily Mirror* readers as much as the slighter political emphasis of the paper itself, that determines the comparative stability of this group of readers. Although the figures here are small and rather unreliable it seems likely that not only the Right-ward drift, but also political instability and uncertainty is most pronounced amongst readers of the *Daily Herald* and *News Chronicle, the two most politically conscious dailies of Liberal or Left opinions.*

Of the Right-wing dailies, the *Daily Express* and *Daily Telegraph* show the strongest tendency to recruit Conservatives from one-time Labour and Liberal voters; and of the three bigger Conservative dailies (*Daily Express, Daily Mail* and *Daily Telegraph*) only the last shows any tendency on the part of its readers to drift in the reverse political direction. *Daily Mail* readers, least politically interested of all the more Conservative readerships, once again are most stable and least inclined in any way to change their political outlook.

One extract from Mass-Observation file material is some information collected in 1942, at the time of the official warning to the *Daily Mirror.* A small-sized sample of people distributed all over the country were asked what they thought of the warning; the *indirect* method of questioning was mostly used, in which the question was brought up informally in the course of casual conversation, and the contact did not know he was being interviewed. This method is more likely to get a near approach to private opinion than when the question is asked directly and formally to strangers. Results, broken down by the daily paper read, are summarized in Table 34[1]:

TABLE 34

Percentage of readers of these papers in favour of the Daily Mirror *warning:*

Daily Paper	%
The Times	53
Daily Express	45
Daily Telegraph	38
News Chronicle	25
Daily Mirror	12

(*N.B.*—Although *Daily Herald* readers were very few, *none* were in favour of the warning.)

[1] The sample was disproportionately weighted with middle-class people. This does not matter much in so far as the purpose of the survey was chiefly just to obtain newspaper correlations, but it does mean that *Daily Herald* readers were too few for statistical mention. *Daily Mail* and *Daily Graphic* readers had also to be excluded, again because with a sample that was unrepresentative the numbers concerned were too few.

It is interesting to relate these results to the editorial policy of each paper with regard to the warning. The *Daily Telegraph* was the only paper whole-heartedly to support the warning, and against it were *The Times*, *Daily Express*, *News Chronicle* and, naturally, the *Daily Mirror* itself. Yet only a third of all *Daily Telegraph* readers were in favour of the warning, fewer than amongst the readers of either *The Times* or *Daily Express*. It seems fairly clear that the immediate editorial attitude of the papers had very little influence on their readers; but the position of the *Daily Telegraph* and of *The Times* is difficult to understand. The majority of *Daily Telegraph* readers were Conservative, their paper was whole-heartedly *in favour of* the *Daily Mirror* warning—yet nearly half of them held opinions differing from their paper's editorial. Of *Times* readers, on the other hand, only two out of five were Conservative, their paper did not agree with the warning—and yet more than half of them approved of it themselves. It seems clear that another factor other than those either of personal politics or editorial influence was helping to shape opinion on this score. Were *Times* readers *emotionally* inclined towards the possible suppression of what may have seemed to them a frivolous and unruly paper? whilst readers of the *Daily Telegraph* for some reason inclined towards the opposite attitude, rejecting the guidance of their paper as well as of their own politics? The position of the *Daily Express* is much more easily understandable, since similar proportion of readers were Conservative, and favoured the warning; but even so it is interesting that as many as 45 per cent should have taken up a position directly opposite that of the paper they read every day. Results generally make it clear that resistance, political as well as more purely emotional, may play havoc with a paper's editorial influence on its readers' opinions.

A third investigation on a similar point concerns the question of Capital Punishment. In 1948, at the time of the Parliamentary discussion of the suspension of the death penalty, Mass-Observation made a large-scale National survey of opinion on this subject, involving the street interviewing of 6,000 people.[1] Throughout the

[1] This survey was made on behalf of the *Daily Telegraph*.

investigation daily paper reading, amongst other factors, was related to opinion on capital punishment, in order to find out how far opinions of this type were influenced by the Press:

TABLE 35

Percentage of readers of these daily papers approving the suspension of the Death Penalty:

Daily Paper	%
Daily Worker	71
Manchester Guardian	32
News Chronicle	23
The Times	21
Daily Herald	18
Daily Telegraph	15
Daily Mirror	10
Daily Graphic	10
Daily Mail	10
Daily Express	9

Editorially opposed to the suspension of the Death Penalty were the *Daily Telegraph, Daily Express, Daily Mail* and *Daily Graphic.* Yet, with the single exception of the *Daily Worker,* the majority of readers of *every* paper are against the suspension. *It is clear that there is a very wide discrepancy here between editorial and readers' opinions: and that on the whole the Press has had little opinion-forming influence on this issue at least.*

The position of the *Daily Mirror* in this table is particularly interesting. *Daily Mirror* readers are almost least inclined of all readership groups to favour suspension, less favourable even than readers of *Daily Telegraph,* and no more favourable than readers of *Daily Mail* and *Daily Graphic,* each of which took up editorially the opposite position to that of the *Daily Mirror.* Our Capital Punishment survey as a whole showed that two of the main factors determining opinion on this issue were education and political outlook—Labour people and the higher education groups were each most inclined to favour suspension. *It is clear that the very working-class composition of the* Daily Mirror *readership is a much stronger factor in shaping their opinion than the line taken up by the paper that they read.* The *Daily Herald* readership, equally working-class, is less resistant to its paper's editorial discussion because of its very strong element of organized Labour, but even so, *Daily Herald* readers are less in sympathy with suspension than readers of the other papers (except the *Daily Mirror*) editorially in favour of this change.

As a further example of what may happen to opinion when readers are strongly resistant to their paper's editorial line, it should be noted that *Daily Mirror* readers tend most of all readership groups to express mixed feelings, or to give no opinion at all. It is clear that readers can exhibit a strong resistance to the line taken editorially by their paper, particularly when it is an issue, which they feel affects themselves personally.

Another example of a failure of editorial influence concerns a *Daily Express* attempt to steer public opinion in a direction which it refused to take. During the first few months of the war preparations were being made for rationing but the scheme had not yet been put into operation; this period, which saw an intensive anti-rationing Press campaign, also produced an increase in public opinion favouring rationing. Closer analysis of attitudes showed that people felt rationing to be necessary from a national point of view, and also believed that it would mean a fair method of distributing commodities which were already in short supply. In this way they were able to ignore propaganda which conflicted with their own personal understanding of the situation.[1]

In the course of the present newspaper survey, an attempt was made to investigate opinion on an issue of international politics where newspaper editorial policy was sharply divided. As subject for this the Marshall Plan was chosen, since this is a question on which two daily papers, the *Daily Express* and *Daily Worker*, take up a position in opposition to the usual newspaper line.

[1] Tom Harrisson, writing in the 1940 publication, *War Begins at Home*, observed 'when the plan to ration butter and bacon was announced, *Daily Express* posters all over the country demanded "Stop Rationing!" The Beaverbrook Press launched thereafter an immense campaign against rationing. By selecting reports and by headline emphasis, they gave a highly inaccurate impression both of the facts of food supplies and of people's feelings on the subject. They were largely instrumental in stimulating several bewildering (for the mass) delays in rationing. But a large majority of the people, in all classes, was decidedly in favour of rationing'. *And the proportion was larger after the Beaverbrook campaign than before it.*

Results are not startling:

TABLE 36

Percentage of readers of these dailies who approve or disapprove of the Marshall Plan[1]:

Opinion	Daily Express %	Daily Mirror %	Daily Herald %	Daily Mail %	News Chronicle %	Daily Telegraph %	Daily Graphic %
Approve	62	60	66	72	73	80	71
Disapprove	12	7	6	8	7	17	5
Don't know	26	33	28	20	20	3	24

The *Daily Telegraph* sample was small, so that sampling errors may partly account for the unusually high proportions deviating from their paper's editorial policy. Apart from the *Daily Telegraph* (and excluding *Daily Worker* readers, too few for accuracy), *Daily Express* readers are most opposed to the Marshall Plan. *But even so 62 per cent of all* Daily Express *readers are in favour of the Marshall Plan, whilst their paper editorially disapproves of it. Two* Daily Express *readers in every three take up the opposite position to that of their paper, and only one in eight agree with it.* It is clear that editorial influence here is very slight, probably particularly so because to the majority of *Daily Express* readers the paper is suggesting an outlook difficult to reconcile with its own long-term Conservative policy, as well as with the Conservatism of most of its readers. Past Mass-Observation surveys have indicated that newspaper influence is much more difficult to exercise when it involves the short-term instilling of relatively new ideas, rather than merely the confirmation and reinforcement of old ones.

It is clear that in home affairs at least the discrepancy between editorial views and reader opinions can be very wide. This emerges from our material on issues such as the *Daily Mirror* warning, the suspension of the Death Penalty, and rationing; in each of these three cases people's personal feelings were sufficiently decisive to withstand the influence of their daily paper, when its views differed from their own. Only on the issue of the Marshall Plan is the discrepancy between newspaper and reader views slighter—with the exception of

[1] People were first asked whether they had heard of the Marshall Plan, and those who had not were excluded from further questioning.

Daily Express readers who diverge in the direction of more orthodox Conservative views. The Marshall Plan is a question of international rather than purely home affairs, superficially much further divorced from the immediate practical life of ordinary people than the home issues of rationing, capital punishment, etc.; for that reason personal views, vague and ill-defined, are less likely to come into conflict with those read in the paper, which is therefore left to wield a correspondingly wider influence upon opinion.

The Marshall Plan is one step removed from everyday life, even though for the more discerning it is at the very least a political matter with no slight personal significance. Further removed from the practical life of ordinary people is the field of international relations, and here our survey material indicates that newspaper influence is considerably stronger. To check up on this point, we asked people how they felt about Americans and Russians; *results in both cases showed only relatively slight discrepancies between newspaper readers and their papers' editorial views.*[1]

Close as the relation is between editorial views and reader opinion in the matter of foreign affairs, minor discrepancies do, however, occur. One of these is a tendency amongst *Daily Express* readers to feel more friendly towards Americans, than their paper—perhaps less orthodoxly Conservative than its readers—appears in its editorials. Another relatively slight discrepancy between paper and reader is the fact that the readership group of *The Times* and *News Chronicle* are friendlier towards the Americans, and less friendly towards the Russians, not only than the editorial of the paper they read, but also in relation to the number of Conservatives amongst themselves. Both groups of readers tend to be more thoughtful and better educated than usual, and are therefore possibly more inclined to criticism; but this does not explain the fact that in both cases their bias is in a Right-wing direction. Does the explanation lie in the *middle-class* character of *Times* readers, combined with the *middle-class* background of most of the intellectual and semi-intellectual amongst readers of the *News Chronicle*? It seems quite possible that

[1] Tables are given in full in Appendix III.

the unconscious influence of class seeps through into that of politics, leading towards resistance to the paper's editorial policy where it seems pro-Russian, and accepting it less reluctantly where it is friendly towards America.

But on the whole the similarity between daily paper editorial and reader views, in the matter of foreign affairs, is very pronounced. In Sunday papers there is again a close relationship, this time with the outstanding exception of the *News of the World*; readers of this paper rank amongst readers of the more Leftish Sunday papers, both in their friendliness to the Russians and their unfriendliness (relatively) to the Americans. It has already been seen that the *News of the World* is read almost entirely for its gossip or features, so that it is not surprising that its readers (the majority of whom themselves have Labour sympathies) remain out of touch with its political views.

How far is the overall similarity between newspaper views on foreign affairs and their readers' opinions on the same subject, a *causal* relationship? To some extent it is just a matter of people choosing their paper primarily for its politics—a common occurrence as will be seen in the next chapter. But it is also possible that, once chosen for its politics, the paper in its turn has a backwash influence on the reader's views. One indication that this is the case, is the fact that people who do *not* read daily papers show quite a distinct pattern of opinion of their own. Non-readers are relatively as unfriendly to the Americans as readers of the *Daily Herald* (least friendly of all), and friendlier towards the Russians than any of the newspaper reading groups at all, even the *Daily Herald* and *Daily Mirror*. Yet as a group non-readers are politically less Labour than readers of either of these Leftish papers, and it seems likely that their tendency to think well of the Russians is to some extent a 'natural state' of feeling, as it exists more or less uninfluenced by Press views and opinion.[1]

---

[1] This may, of course, also be partly due to the fact that some people read no daily paper simply because they are cynical about the impartiality of the Press generally—and such people are more likely to belong to the intellectual Left than to the Right; but the widespread lack of interest and apathy characterizing non-readers, together with the fact that they are predominantly women, makes this unlikely as anything more than a small part of the explanation.

This is the more likely in light of other material on Mass-Observation files. Repeated check-ups on popular attitudes to the Russians from 1938 onwards have indicated a deep-seated desire to think well of them, even at times when Press opinion of that country was at its lowest.[1] The same conclusion emerges from present day tests of opinion. Since the end of the war unfavourable feeling about the Russians has been slowly mounting, but always reluctantly. Reports of interviews, particularly informal interviews more likely to give a glimpse of people's most deep-seated feelings, constantly give the impression that any encouragement given to think favourably of the Russians would be accepted whole-heartedly. In light of this, it is not surprising that whilst the Press continues in its present anti-Russian strain, people who do not come into regular contact with it are so much more pro-Russian than newspaper readers.

It is clear that although people tend to resist newspaper influences that lead them in a direction they are not disposed to follow, newspaper influence on opinion does certainly exist, particularly in the long-term sense of reinforcement of opinions already held. This is likely to be particularly pronounced in that most people—as the next chapter will show—choose their paper primarily for its politics; and since most readers feel themselves to be aware of, and in sympathy with, their paper's bias, they tend critically to be off their guard, to some extent at least. Following up this point we asked people which political party they thought their daily paper supported. *As many as two-thirds of the whole newspaper reading sample gave more or less the right reply.*

It is amongst these relatively knowledgeable readers that the newspaper is most likely to influence opinion. Over a long-term period, the newspapers' influence can be very pronounced (especially, as has been seen, in the sphere of foreign affairs); the process by which readers' opinion is eased along in its natural direction may not only take the form of very strong reinforcement, but may also border on the formation of new ideas, in that it sows seeds and implants

[1] See articles in the *Public Opinion Quarterly*, Fall 1947; the *Political Quarterly*, January 1947; *News Review*, July 29, 1948.

suggestions on points to which people have up to now given next to no thought. Provided that these are, at least superficially, compatible with the reader's own outlook, they stand a good chance of being incorporated amongst his attitudes and opinions.

The reverse side of this picture is also of importance. Newspaper influence fails sometimes through reader-resistances, sometimes through reader-apathy; as an illustration of this second point, it is instructive to know that one reader in five has no idea which political party his daily paper supports and still more are wide of the mark. Picture paper readers most of all are politically in the dark about their newspaper; one-third of all *Daily Mirror* readers do not know which party their paper supports (5 per cent attribute it to the Conservative party). One-fifth of all *Daily Mail* readers, and nearly as many of the readers of the *Daily Express*, do not know what are their papers' politics. Roughly one *News Chronicle* reader in ten believes that paper to be Conservative and 7 per cent of all *Daily Mail* readers think they are reading a Labour paper. Women are particularly ignorant of their paper's political outlook, and class differences are consistently very pronounced; readers' awareness of their paper's politics increases steeply with social class. *But it is clear that newspaper political influence has been slight at least amongst these worst-informed readership groups, and that there must be a relatively high proportion of readers who just do not read political news and comment; earlier results have shown that this is, in fact, the case.*

Impact of Film Reviews

Picture-goers were asked to recall the name of the last film they had seen, the name of the film critic in their daily paper, and what he had said about this film.

Of the overwhelming majority who say they go to the pictures at all, about three-quarters could remember the name of the last film they had seen; differences between newspaper readerships, however, are slight in this respect, and also in ability to recall the name of the film critic.

There are similarly slight differences between newspapers in the extent to which their readers can recall the content of film reviews:

TABLE 37

Percentage of readers of these daily papers able to recall what their paper's film critic said about the last film that they saw:

Daily Paper	%
Daily Herald	10
Daily Express	9
News Chronicle	8
Daily Mail ⎱ Daily Telegraph ⎰	7
Daily Mirror ⎱ Daily Graphic ⎰	5

(Total, all daily papers: 7 per cent.)

The most important fact emerging from this table is the evidence that most people do not, consciously at all events, choose their films according to what they read of them in the daily paper. Only 7 per cent of the readers of all daily papers can give the name of their film critic, and the same percentage is able to recall what the critic said of the last film that they took the trouble to go and see. *Film reviews can have little conscious influence on the picture-going activity of the daily paper public.* How far they have a more subtle influence, determining attitudes whose origins become forgotten, it is impossible as yet to say; but specially designed penetrative research should be able to clarify this point to some extent.

In so far as film reviews are successful in conditioning opinion and behaviour at an articulate level, it is chiefly amongst middle-class people that they have this influence. Very few unskilled working-class people can name their paper's film critic, and not many more can remember what he has said.

TABLE 38

Percentage of people in these class groups able correctly to recall the name of their paper's film critic:

	%
Middle-class	17
Artisan-class	6
Unskilled working-class	2

(Total, all classes : 7 per cent)

10 per cent of all middle-class picture-goers were able to recall what their paper's film critic said about the last film they had seen,

against 8 per cent of artisan-class people and 5 per cent of those of the unskilled working-class. Adding this to the fact that the middle-classes are also a little more able to name the last film that they saw, it seems clear that this group is most consciously and discriminatingly interested in films, and also that the film critic caters for a reading public that is heavily weighted with middle-class readers.

The Impact of the Sports Page

If film reviews proved to have little effect on opinion and behaviour, it was still possible that the impact of the sports page might be stronger. To test this we asked people who were at all accustomed to filling in football pool coupons whether they used their paper's pool forecasts. Once again differences between newspapers were very slight, although this time increase in social status made it less likely that newspaper forecasts would be used:

TABLE 39

Percentage of readers of these daily papers[1] who say they use their paper's pool forecasts:

Daily Paper	%
Daily Herald	40
News Chronicle	39
Daily Express	35
Daily Mirror ⎫ Daily Mail ⎭	33

(*Total for all daily papers: 34 per cent.*)

One person in three fills in football coupons regularly (chiefly men, and working-class people rather more than the middle-class). Of these one-third, again, say they make use of their paper's pool forecast; this time there is no difference between the sexes. *Thus one daily paper reader in every nine fills in football pool coupons, and in doing so uses his paper's forecast: roughly one in ten goes to the pictures and in addition can remember what his paper's film critic said about the last film that he saw.* But the impact of pool forecasts must be regarded as considerably greater than that of film reviews. One pools enthusiast in three, compared with only one picture-goer in thirteen is affected by what he reads in his daily paper. And finally, since men

[1] As only a third of the whole sample said that they filled in football pool coupons regularly, daily paper groups dwindled correspondingly, and only those with the biggest readerships could be included.

fill in football coupons more than women, and working-class people not only fill them in more than the middle-classes, but also turn more to newspaper forecasts, it is clear that the sports page, in so far as football pools are concerned, caters chiefly for men, and for working- rather than middle-class people.

Sceptical Readers

Mass-Observation Panel is of particular value in showing trends and changes of attitude that take place over a period of a number of years. Membership of this group remains more or less stable, and even where old members retire and new ones are recruited, the self-selection factor operates in such a way that the group as a whole does not perceptibly alter from year to year.

In 1940, 1941, 1942, 1944, 1946 and 1948, members of this group were asked to rank a number of possible opinion forming influences, in the order in which they felt their opinion to be formed by them. The results cannot be expected to give any reliable indication of the actual influence of each of these factors. But the order in which people arrange them, and especially *changes* in this order, are of interest in the light that they throw on attitudes to these media. The actual in-fluence of the Press is likely to decline with any drop in its prestige, and it is this latter development that our Panel material is reflecting.

Table 40 summarizes the results:

TABLE 40

Mass-Observation Panel rankings of twelve opinion-forming media in these years:[1]

	1940	1941	1942	1944	1946	1948
Personal experience	5	2	2	2	1	1
Own opinion	1	1	1	1	2	3
Books	2	3	3	3	3	2
Friends and family	4	6	5	4	4	4
NEWSPAPERS	3	4	4	5	5	5
Recent travel and history	6	7	6	7	6	6
Radio	7	5	7	6	7	7
Meetings	9	11	8	9	8	8
Pamphlets	8	8	9	8	9	9
Films	10	9	10	10	10	10
Posters	12	12	12	12	11	12
Public information and leaflets	11	10	11	11	12	11

[1] The categories which people were offered for ranking are not regarded as perfect. They were drawn up in the first place for a special purpose, and have not been changed since as any alteration would forfeit their value as an indication of trends.

During these eight years there has been a consistent tendency for newspapers to sink in people's estimate as an opinion forming influence, a decline which has maintained itself even up to the present. In 1940 only books and people's own judgment were put before newspapers. By 1941 'personal experience' had also taken precedence of newspapers, and it is clear that people were becoming more wary of Press opinions, and more anxious to think things out for themselves. By 1944 'friends and family' had joined the three factors in a more trusted position than that of newspapers, and it seems likely that as the latter fell more and more into disrepute, readers were trying to replace the one-time opinion-forming influence of the Press with the fruits of discussion as well as by attaching more importance to book-reading, and by relying more and more on their own judgment and experience.

It is especially interesting that as people became more reluctant to submit to the influence of the Press they seem to have turned more to themselves and their friends, and to books from which they could select with a wide range of choice; *there is no increased tendency to rely on other opinion forming agencies such as radio and films which might be subject to the same defects as are apparent in newspapers.*

Reasons for this growing distrust of newspapers have been emerging throughout this report. The war intensified the feeling that Press news is biased, and inaccurate; in addition many people regard newspapers as sensational and indifferent to their true function as purveyors of *news*.

'Some of the headlines in the *Daily Mirror* are misleading. They give people the wrong impression.' (*Unskilled worker*, 34.)

This west country working-man, doubtful of the truthfulness of his newspaper's headlines, is displaying only an embryo scepticism. It is a far cry from his suspicions to the laconic disillusionment that is becoming increasingly frequent. More and more newspaper readers are wary of believing what they read, and less and less are they inclined to think that there is any newspaper at all that can really be trusted:

'There's something I dislike about all papers, and that is that they don't tell the truth. . . . There's so much stuff not worth looking at, adverts, scandal, and all that stuff that isn't news.' (*Unskilled worker, 35, reads* Daily Mirror.)

'All newspapers are the same.' (*Unskilled worker, 44, reads* Daily Express.)

'The main thing I like about *The Times* is that I dislike other papers more.' (*University lecturer, 39.*)

But, finally, it must be emphasized that though doubts about the trustworthiness of newspapers, and consequent resistance to their opinion-forming influence have grown considerably during the last ten years, *such scepticism still, at its conscious level at all events, probably remains more or less a minority attitude.* The majority of people read the political parts of their paper sketchily and with little thought of criticizing. In this way they absorb its outlook and political trend all the more, just because they are reading uncritically, and because on most issues the newspaper is unlikely to come into conflict with their own opinions, which anyway are less clearly defined. The opinion-forming influence of the Press is at its strongest largely in that it is a subtle, almost imperceptible, process, but also in that most people feel that they are reading opinions which long ago they perhaps subconsciously identified with their own. The war shook people out of this lethargy to some extent; but it still remains a powerful factor in leaving the way free for Fleet Street influence on the formation of public opinion.

XVI: THE PROCESS OF CHOICE

'We've had the *Express* ever since it was first printed. My father had a copy of the first edition. I take it because Dad had it, and I'd got used to it. I don't know that there's anything I *particularly* like about it; I could quarrel with it, often. But if I buy another paper I always go back to it.' (*Woman, 60, artisan class, Labour voter.*)

Up to this point we have discussed attitudes to various sections of newspapers and the impact of the paper as a whole, but we have seldom referred to one of the most important factors of all—the motives for the original *choice* of paper. It has been necessary to leave this until the last in order to have clarified the relative importance of various aspects of newspapers. During the course of this chapter, however, many subjects already discussed will have to be referred to again, though from a different angle.

What is the attraction that ties people to one paper, even though they have no outstanding reason for taking it and, like this woman, are often at variance with its views? How common, anyway, is this sort of tie between paper and reader? And how far do people consciously and deliberately select one paper rather than another? It is these and similar questions that this chapter sets out to discuss.

For some people, like the woman quoted above, the element of conscious choice in newspaper reading is very slight. Occasionally—but not usually—this is a matter of indifference. Some people feel that all newspapers are the same, with little or nothing to choose between them; this sort of attitude, moreover, appears as much amongst people who seem more or less satisfied with their paper, as amongst those who are cynical and disillusioned. One of our interviews, for instance, discovered a farmer, with an income of between £600–£1,000 a year, who could not even think of the name of the paper he bought every day:

'One comes every day, but I don't know which it is.'

And this *News of the World* reader finds nothing to distinguish her paper from any other:

'It's a job to say, I don't know, they're all the same.' (*Unskilled working-class woman, 35.*)

Some people seem to take newspapers with little concern for what is actually inside them:

'I read the *Evening Standard*. I buy it to keep me occupied when I'm travelling home in the bus at night, so as not to look at the fellow sitting opposite.' (*Middle-class man, 45.*)

'Reading passes the morning, to tell the truth.' (*Unskilled working-class woman, 22.*)

For people such as these the process of choice is more likely to depend on chance factors, or semi-conscious preferences, rather than on any more clear-cut reasoning. One person in every twenty, asked what he particularly liked about his daily paper, could think of nothing to reply.[1] And amongst readers of every other sort of paper, Sundays, evenings and local weeklies, the proportion of negative replies was about twice as high.

This does not, of course, mean that all of these are indifferent about which paper they actually read. It is often difficult, particularly for less adequately educated people, to find an immediate answer to a direct and unexpected question from a stranger; this is especially the case when it concerns a point which may at one time been given some thought, but which now has become merged into a mass of background habits and unquestioned attitudes. As a result of a small-scale 'family' questionnaire designed to supplement our national survey, it became particularly clear that controlled probing, with a number of differently framed questions touching similar points, often produced positive answers where negative ones were given in the first place; people, for instance, who first of all said they did not know why they preferred one newspaper, would later give reasons for taking their own rather than any other. To some extent, this may, of course, represent an indifference for which rationalizations have been hastily provided, or possibly a polite desire to please

---

[1] These, and other results concerning what people like about their paper, are given in tabular form in Appendix III.

the interviewer; but for the most part, in this case, it seems to be either the product of slow thinking, or the sorting out of long-forgotten attitudes.

It is especially difficult for many people to reply to questions which involve the spontaneous mention of specific reasons for choice—such as, for example, 'sport', 'features', 'political angle', and so on; questions which ask simply for the expression of an attitude (approval or disapproval, for instance) can be answered relatively easily even when no conscious thought has been given to the point. Thus 'don't know' answers to the questions on what people like about their newspaper must be regarded as an almost certainly exaggerated estimate of indifference.

Discrimination

Except for a few extreme cases, some of which have already been quoted, *most people have some reason for reading the paper that they do.* Even when they are as vague as this:

'The *Daily Herald*. It's very nice. There's nothing in particular.' (*Woman, unskilled working-class*, 62.)

'I read the *Express*. I like the paper in general.' (*Woman, unskilled working-class*, 40.)

Even in such cases people are often reluctant to change to any other paper. The key to the problem is, quite clearly, the phrase 'in general'. The reader's preference for one particular paper is based on a complexity of different points almost impossible to unravel. He likes a paper that he is used to, that he knows well enough to be able to find his way around in. He likes a paper that does not clash with his outlook, and which as far as possible, indulges his interests. Some prefer a paper which is quick and easy to read, and which dresses its news up into an attractive and gossiping form; others enjoy the sense of reliability. Some choose a paper which satisfies their desire either for an aggressive approach to outside matters, or for a more stolid, stable one. Even factors such as size of paper, and type of print are important and affect different people in quite different ways.

It is certainly impossible to rank the factors determining choice of newspaper according to their degree of influence, or even to point to certain factors as the chief decisive ones. Even to separate certain factors from the rest is an arbitrary and questionable process, that runs the risk of divorcing the whole problem from reality. For the most part all that can be done is to attempt to show how far certain vaguely defined factors seem to influence the majority of people; and also, in even broader terms, to indicate how far newspapers differ one from another in their readers' sensitivity to these factors.

It may, however, be pointed out at this stage that in our supplementary small-scale London survey in which people were asked why they first started taking their present morning paper one-quarter mentioned the paper's politics, one-fifth the news and the way it is presented, one-tenth the sports items, and one-tenth the comics and cartoons. Not many people mentioned more than one reason. Much of this may be rationalization or simplification, but the *order* of importance is probably not incorrect. There is in the first place no doubt that one of the biggest influences is that of politics and class.

Politics on Weekdays

At least 40 per cent of the readers of every daily paper support one single political party. The *Daily Mail* and *Daily Telegraph* each have a majority of Conservative readers, and a minority of from 26 per cent to 9 per cent Labour. The *Daily Mirror* has a similar majority of Labour voters, and the *News Chronicle* readership is 50 per cent Labour. *The Times* is nearly as Conservative in its readership as the *Daily Graphic* and *Daily Express*, and has a similar one in four minority of Labour voters, and one in seven Liberal. These last three are the only papers without a majority of their readers supporting any one party. The *Daily Mirror* has the highest proportion of politically uninterested or unattached readers, and at the other extreme *Daily Herald* readers are easily the most solidly one-Party, with a minority of only 9 per cent Conservatives or Liberals.[1]

[1] See Table 45 in Appendix III.

It is impossible to separate the influence of class and politics here; each works to the same end, and usually in conjunction with the other. Verbatims bring out very clearly the strength of the class elements:

'I read the *Herald*. I like to read about the working man.' (*Unskilled worker*, 60.)

'The *Mirror*, I thought it was the most popular paper and you get good articles in it. And also it's a paper for the working-class man.' (*Labouring man*, 25.)

'I like the *Herald* because it gives me the Labour news, the financial news don't interest me. The others are all capitalist press, and they're not interested in the working-class and what they're going to get.' (*Park sweeper*, 55.)

'My husband likes the *Telegraph* because it's a Conservative paper, and you can rely on it, really—you don't get these screaming headlines.' (*Unskilled working-class housewife*, 40.)

Class, in its political sense particularly, is most often mentioned by *Daily Herald* and *Daily Mirror* readers, and least often by readers of *The Times* and *Telegraph*. And of a small, but representative sample interviewed in London, one person in four mentioned politics as his original reason for taking his present daily: in view of the often very generalized nature of the factor the same reason is likely to be implicit in the replies of many others. The skilled worker, for instance, who started taking the *Daily Herald* because:

'I like the general political outlook, and I like the attitude of the paper altogether. I'm used to it.'

—is not necessarily very different in his attitude from those, often less articulate, who say they take their paper for its news, because they like it, or because they are used to it. It has already been seen that only one person in every five is ignorant of his paper's political line. The fact that only one in ten of our National sample specifies politics as one of the things he likes about his morning paper may at first sight seem to point in the opposite direction, but probably serves only to show how very fundamental and deep-set in its influence this factor is. The fact remains that three-quarters of both Conservatives and Labour sympathisers read a daily paper which reflects their own bias, *and it seems reasonably certain that politics is usually more important than anything else in deciding which daily paper people read.*

On the other hand, if politics are the most frequent factor governing choice, they are not always the primary one. Not everyone even knows what his paper's politics consist of, and many are totally out of sympathy with the views of a paper which they still continue to read. Among the supporters of every political party there is quite a substantial minority reading a paper with different politics to their own. Seven Conservatives out of every ten, for instance, read Conservative papers, but one in four reads either the *Daily Herald, News Chronicle* or *Daily Mirror*—chiefly the latter. The split is rather less pronounced in the case of Labour supporters, one in five of whom read Conservative papers (*Daily Express, Daily Mail, Daily Graphic* or *Daily Telegraph*). Liberals are, understandably, most divided; less than a third read either *The Times* or *News Chronicle*, over half read Conservative papers, and about one in six either the *Daily Herald* or *Daily Mirror*.

In some cases a paper is read in full awareness of its uncongenial politics—as, for instance, in the case of this middle-aged artisan, who likes to read the *Daily Express*. When a paper is read primarily for something quite distinct from its political views the fact that its political outlook does not altogether coincide with that of its reader, becomes more or less irrelevant:

'I don't always agree with its views, but I think the *Express* presents the news in an interesting way, which in my opinion makes the paper more interesting than any other. I like its style, it's an easily read paper.'

On the other hand, the one in five ignorant of their paper's politics shows that the morning paper is by no means always associated with politics; it is partly this minority that reads papers with whose politics they are out of sympathy.

The influence of politics varies very much in importance from one paper to another. The *Daily Herald* and *News Chronicle* particularly are liked for their political line and, as has already been seen, a quarter of all *News Chronicle* readers give this as one of their reasons for taking the *News Chronicle* (as compared to one in five of *Daily*

Herald readers, one in six of the *Daily Telegraph* and one in every ten of the *Daily Mail*). *Daily Express* readers come near the bottom of the list with one in seventeen, and only three in a hundred of picture paper readers read them for their political views. *Times* readers mention politics least of all.[1]

It seems clear enough that the *Daily Herald* is most outstandingly read for its politics, and that readers of this paper are most of all influenced by their class and political outlook, particularly the former, in making their choice of paper. In so far as the other dailies are concerned politics operate less directly as a determining factor, and are probably influential only within the wider set-up of general background of interest. Although most people choose a morning paper which suits their own class and political outlook, once politically incompatible papers have been excluded other narrower factors may determine the final choice, and the political element may be more or less accepted and forgotten. Politics, for instance, may give preference to the *Daily Mirror* rather than the *Daily Graphic*, but choice will still fall upon a picture paper:

'We read the *Daily Sketch* until we became Labour, and then we gave it up and took the *Mirror*.' (*Middle-class woman*, 20.)

Class, education and 'serious' interests decide that people shall read either the *Daily Telegraph* or *Times*; politics may determine which. Similarly, readers of the three popular papers other than the *Daily Herald* are all drawn from a more or less standard background, but factors such as sport and special features play a big part in choice between the *Daily Express* and *Daily Mail*, and, to a lesser extent, the *News Chronicle*.

The position of the *News Chronicle* seems slightly ambiguous; for some of its readers it has a strong political draw, whilst at the same time there is a high proportion who take it in spite of their political opinions, and are obviously finding some other attraction. Mass-Observation Panel material clarifies the position of the *News Chronicle* reader to a certain extent; it is easily the most popular daily paper amongst members of the Panel group, nearly half of whom read it,

[1] See Table 43 in Appendix III.

whilst nearly a fifth read this and no other paper. One section of *News Chronicle* readers is quite clearly made up of this type of serious-minded, politically and socially 'progressive' middle-class person—the higher income parallel of the *Daily Herald* reader—who reads this paper mostly because he consciously agrees with its views:

> 'I am a member of the Labour Party, but the *Herald* is so dull and un-appetising. The *Chronicle*, I feel, presents the news fairly, presents both sides of the controversial questions . . . is generally sane and open-minded in its outlook to important current affairs. . . .' (*Young man, Panel member.*)

The other, less intelligent, aspect of the *News Chronicle* readership is more or less unrepresented in our Panel group, but even in this middle-class group, there is a tendency to select the paper for its presentation and general 'tone' as much as for its political angle; the two aspects are, of course, very closely inter-related:

> 'The *Chronicle* is neither pro- nor anti-Government. It speaks with rather more restraint than the other cheap dailies, and is less obviously grinding an axe. The general tone, and layout do not offend me, as the *Mail*, *Express* and *Herald* do.' (*Clerk, Panel member.*)

On the whole, the News Chronicle *more than any other daily paper except the* Daily Herald, *is deliberately chosen for its political views.* But in that this factor is very often deeply embedded in a mass of others, usually less important, it is quite typical of the process of choice in so far as daily papers are concerned.

Politics on Sundays

In Sunday papers news interest gives way to features, and politics play a correspondingly reduced role. As a result, the political aspect of readership differences is less clear-cut, and people are less inclined to confine themselves to newspapers expressing similar views to their own. Nearly every second Labour supporter, for instance, reads the *News of the World*, whereas only one in every twelve or thirteen selects the only Left-wing Sunday, *Reynolds News*.

Since people are so often more or less indifferent to news content in their Sunday reading, incompatible politics can more easily be overlooked; it is likely that many people have not even noticed what sort of politics the *News of the World* possesses—because they are almost exclusively interested in the gossip and other features:

'I can't remember why I first started reading the *News of the World*. I don't read it all. I always do the dress competition and the crossword. I've been doing them for years now. I've never won anything—I would have given it up if it wasn't for the competitions.' (*Housewife, 50, skilled working-class.*)

It is clear that in Sunday papers politics can be overlooked in the search for entertaining and exclusive feature material. It has already been seen that very few people mention the Sunday paper's politics as something that they particularly like about it, and equally few give this as their original reason for taking the paper. Only in *Reynolds News*, whose readership is most nearly one-Party (three-quarters are either Labour or Communist)[1] and whose readers most often mention its political views as something they like, do politics and social class seem to play a large part in determining people's choice; whilst amongst readers of the *Sunday Times* and *Observer* it seems likely that the same factor again plays a large if less consciously decisive part. For the rest, although almost every paper does in effect cater for a readership the bulk of whom fall into its own political category, this seems to be largely a matter of class-attraction, and politics is just one of a great many other almost equally minor factors.

Presentation

Closely allied to the political factor, is the feeling that a paper is better because it is unbiased. If a paper fits in with its readers' own views, it will be regarded as reliable and truthful, and if not, it is assumed to be politically biased. News Chronicle *and* Daily Herald *readers most often mention lack of bias as a reason for their preferences, just as they most often prefer their paper for its politics.* Picture paper readers, particularly readers of the *Daily Graphic*, make this claim least often of all, probably not because they think their paper is biased, but rather because they tend to be much less interested in politics. And again, the question of political bias is brought up much

[1] See Table 46 in Appendix III.

less often in respect of Sunday papers.

Absence of sensationalism is mentioned chiefly by readers of the class papers:

'Well, I read the *Telegraph* because I always used to like the *Morning Post*. I like it because it's a good paper, it's not sensational press with the old headlines, not giddy reading, not as laborious as *The Times*. It's something to get your teeth into, I like it.' (*Middle-class woman*, 50.)

'*Interesting news*' (by which gossip is often meant) and light, bright and easy presentation is often a choice-determining factor amongst readers of the picture papers, and the *Daily Express* and *Daily Mail*, but seldom in any of the other dailies. *Daily Graphic* readers particularly often choose this paper because it is quickly and effortlessly read:

'No, there was no reason, really, why I started taking the *Graphic*. In fact all my brothers and sisters, they live the other side of London, and they all have the *Express*—so I don't know why I started having the *Graphic*, except that it has the news briefly told.' (*Labourer*, 30.)

'I like the *Graphic*—well, I get down to the news quick, there's not a lot. It's short and sweet, sort of thing.' (*Builder's manager*, 40.)

The taste for light news and an easy presentation is sometimes frankly escapist:

'What I like about the *News of the World* today is that it sets out to take your mind off present-day troubles, it puts out the lighter side of life, and you can forget about what's happening in Parliament and all that.' (*Fireman*, 30.)

From this point of view *pictures*, too, are often an important advantage, particularly amongst women, and people of a poor educational level:

'The *Mirror*. I took it because I liked the pictures. It's *easy*.' (*Housewife, unskilled working-class*, 25.)

'I read the *Mirror* . . . I had it just to take a paper, no particular reason . . . well, it's the illustrations that I like, and the pictures.' (*Car park attendant*, 60.)

'I like Pip, Squeak and Wilfred, and Jane, and the pictures are a help to you, you don't want to always have to read.' (*Housepainter's wife*, 65.)

Some people enjoy a certain element of aggressiveness in their paper—something which will give them the feeling that evasive facts are being uncovered for them, or that corruptions and inefficiencies are being exposed:

'The *Herald*, well, they give you home truths about most things—and the sporting part is good.' (*Window cleaner*, 40.)

'I like what they call the Live Letter Box, that tells you home truths.' (*Man, cleaner*, 30.)

'One thing I like about the *Express* is the notice they have brought to several things, they raise things in their columns. Like the petrol rationing, done a lot of good that way.' (*Artisan*, 35.)

'I like the *Mirror*, you get little bits and pieces in a nutshell, and they call a spade a spade, and that's why I like it.' (*Club porter*, 45.)

Except in people's enjoyment of scandal, this sort of feeling is not often aroused by Sunday papers, again largely because news interest is so much slighter in Sundays than in dailies.

'Funnies'

Cartoons and comics, and the funny parts of the paper, are chiefly important amongst readers of the *Daily Mirror* and the *Sunday* and *Daily Express*. About one person in ten of our small-scale London survey gave comics as their original reason for taking their present daily, usually the *Daily Mirror*:

'Well, I don't know, I think I started taking the *Mirror* because I was interested in Garth, and the little bits and pieces. Now I have it because I've got to have it. The wife and child say they want it, so I pay for it, and let them have it.' (*Porter*, 45.)

And even where the *Daily Mirror* was not originally taken for its strips, these have often grown into one of the main reasons for liking it now:

'We've taken the *Mirror* since 1940, prior to that we took in the *Daily Sketch* . . . I forget what particular reason it was now, I believe it was something to do with some women's patterns that my wife liked . . . well, myself I like it because the sports page is quite enterprising, and we all clamour for Jane, and the comic strips.' (*Gas fitter*, 30.)

Features

Articles, serial stories, and, apart from cartoons, special features such as reviews, crosswords, fashions, etc., are more often a reason for taking Sundays than dailies. It is impossible to point to any single one of these factors as particularly important:

'We take the *Observer*—it's just the way it's set out, particularly the theatre news and reviews of films.' (*Middle-class man, actor.*)

'I took the *News of the World* because of the crossword puzzles, and the same goes for the *Sunday Chronicle* too.' (*Man, civil servant, 44.*)

'The *Sunday Express*. I used to like some of those articles in it, though I don't think they've been quite so good lately. Nat Gubbins is a favourite of mine.' (*Artisan, 34.*)

'We've had the *Sunday Dispatch* ever since they started publishing *Forever Amber*; that's the real reason I took that paper, I always wanted to read that book, and I couldn't afford to buy it, so when they started publishing it in the *Dispatch* I ordered it. Now they have another serial, and I am reading that.' (*Woman, hotel housekeeper, 55.*)

'The *News of the World* . . . I don't remember why we started having it. But we nearly all read "The Stars", and I like looking down the poultry— I used to keep chickens and ducks. Only one thing I don't like it for . . . it's full of scandal.' (*Housewife, unskilled working-class, 59.*)

As has been suggested earlier, it is just such special features as these that draw people to one Sunday paper rather than another. And, on the whole, the habit element seems to work particularly strongly in Sunday papers, especially in connection with these features. *In the absence of such acute political discrimination as that which occurs amongst dailies, people prefer one Sunday paper to another largely because they like to know their way about its features, and especially when there is one particular feature that has an outstanding attraction for them.*

It is for this very reason that chance is a very strong factor in determining choice of Sunday paper. People may take one paper because their family has always taken it, or because at one time they could not get any other, and so grew into enjoying this one; or since originally taking and getting used to a paper it has not occurred to them to change. Reading through verbatim accounts of interviews imparts a feeling that for many people spontaneously to make a change would be difficult, not only from sheer inertia, but also out of the fondness *grown from habit*, even though, habit apart, other Sunday papers might suit them just as well as their present choice. But once chance or any other influence has precipitated a change people may easily drift into accepting a different Sunday paper:

'We haven't taken the *News of the World* for long—about twelve months. We used to have the *People* before that—then they didn't deliver it one Sunday, but left the *News of the World* instead. And we continued with it—my wife thinks there's more in it.' (*Artisan*, 38.)

But habit is strong enough to ensure that this sort of change does not often take place:

'Oh, I couldn't say *when* we started taking the *News of the World*. I should say for the last twenty years. We always had it at home when I was younger.' (*Electrician*, 45.)

And, to a lesser extent, habit operates as a factor in determining choice of dailies too.

'We have the *Graphic*, it's always been there, it was there when I was a schoolgirl, and I've grown up with it.' (*Mechanic's wife*, 50.)

The Sports Enthusiast

Finally, the influence of sport. One person in every eight or nine mentions sport as something he particularly likes about the morning paper, and one in four mentions reading it. This proportion is considerably higher amongst readers of the popular papers, especially the *Daily Herald*, and much lower amongst class and picture paper readers. In the case of Sunday papers, the *News of the World* is most outstanding, and at the opposite end of the scale, least interested, come the *Sunday Times*, *Sunday Express* and the *Observer*. Sport is an object of more or less equal interest amongst readers of morning, evening and Sunday papers, and is less important to the local weekly reader. In morning papers it is almost the only specific part of the paper occasioning any considerable degree of resentment, one-quarter of the whole sample saying that they never read it, almost exactly the same proportion as that which mentions the sports items as part of their regular morning paper reading routine. Women scarcely mention sport at all, and people of elementary education are more interested than the secondary or university groups. In other words, sport is a semi-specialized topic that is very important to numbers of the men readers of almost every sort of paper; *it is of more or less prime importance to about a fifth of these men readers.*

Even amongst men it is only a small minority that cares for nothing in the morning paper but sport:

'I read the *Express*. I like it for the sports events . . . there's a sports page by Frank Butler, I think it is.' (*Unskilled working man*, 19.)

This boy takes the *Daily Express* in spite of the fact that he dislikes its politics ('. . . It's a Tory paper . . . I'd vote Communist if I was old enough'). It is *only* the sport that interests him, and he takes no other daily. A barrow-boy, interviewed in Pimlico, also takes the *Daily Express* for the same single reason:

'I've had the *Express* about ten years . . . it was more for the sport I used to buy it . . . I like the sport on the back page. That's all I read in it really.' (*Barrow boy*, 24, *Labour voter.*)

But although this young man takes the Daily Express *for its sport alone, he is not only interested in sport.* In addition to the *Daily Express* he takes the *Daily Mirror*, and this time he reads much more of the paper:

'I've had the *Mirror* for about a year . . . I took it to see Jane . . . I like all the facts in the *Mirror*, they're nice and realistic, vivid.'

And for the most part when people take a paper for its sport alone, they read another, like the barrow-boy, for news and features. Most of the people who take only one morning paper, however strong their interest in sport at first appears, seem to read other parts of the paper besides. More often than not the other interests slip out casually during the course of several parallel questions, as a more vague and generalized background to an outstanding sporting interest:

'The *Express* . . . oh, I've had it for years and years—twenty to twenty-five years . . . well, I took it because I fancied the sports features years ago . . . well, there's no particular bit I like, it's just the paper as a whole.' (*General foreman*, 50.)

'I started taking the *Mirror* about twenty years ago—well, because I was particularly fond of sport and there used to be a lot of sport in it. I particularly like the Live Letter Box, and the back page for kiddies.' (*Handyman*, 55.)

For the most part it is only evening papers that may be read exclusively for their sports news alone:

'I like any bloody paper that has the horse racing results in.' (*Waitress*, 30.)

Sunday papers present very much the same sort of picture as dailies; again most sports enthusiasts either take one paper for sport and another for features and general reading, or else read other things in the paper besides sport:

'We've had the *News of the World* and the *People* both for over twenty years now . . . we started taking the *News of the World* because they give you the full account of the whole story, if you're interested in murder cases . . . we like it because you can read the whole week's stories in it of all those bits and pieces in different editions and dailies . . . but we had the *People* because it was a good paper for sports, half of it is sports, whatever sport you follow you gets its results.' (*Tar paver,* 35.)

'We've had the *People* ever since *Lloyds* fell out, I took it over then, it must be more than twenty years . . . well, I don't know what was the cause of my buying it, except that it was a very good paper for news and sport, especially sport . . . I like it because they report the football matches very well, and it's very plain for reading and that.' (*Mechanical repairer,* 50.)

It is clear that some people use sports content as their only criterion in deciding which paper to take. Their numbers are unlikely to exceed the one in ten figure that mentioned sport as their original reason for taking their present daily; but it must be remembered that many others take sport into consideration as a *supplementary* reason—a well-presented and efficient sports page is certainly an important though highly specialized part of the indefinable general appeal that a favourite paper has for its sporting reader. Lastly, enthusiasts are especially critical; where the paper is chosen for its sports content the influence of habit becomes much slighter than usual.

There are, of course, other subsidiary factors which either influence the choice of just a few people, or play a very background part in determining general appeal; pictures, for instance, fall into this category, with smaller items such as crosswords, recipes, advertisements, and so on. But any attempt to single out such minor factors here would be both arbitrary and futile.

Conclusion

On the whole, it seems clear that the major factor determining choice of newspaper is the generalized one of political outlook and class background. For most people this operates in such a way as to narrow the range of choice, with the final decision depending on a complex mass of factors in which individual influences have a varying importance. *But the process is essentially one of elimination rather than of deliberate selection.* In most cases it is extremely hazy and difficult to define, with a heavy emphasis on habit and chance contacts, and on the personal feeling of attachment which grows and spreads itself over the whole paper once people have taken it for any length of time and once they have become accustomed not only to the individuality of its features but also to its peculiarity of presentation and general layout. To answer the questions posed at the beginning of this chapter, the process of choice is for most people only partly conscious, born as it is of the elimination of undesirables. The reader is tied to his paper largely through a half-formulated sympathy of class and outlook, but also by an entanglement of innumerable other small factors grown over with the influence of habit and the attraction of the known and familiar.

XVII: NEWSPAPER BY NEWSPAPER

THROUGHOUT this report the reader may have found himself faced with apparently unco-ordinated references to differences between newspaper readerships. This has been unavoidable since in order to avoid additional confusion it was necessary to subordinate discussion of readers' reactions to newspapers in particular to that of reaction to papers in general. Newspaper differences may, however, be clarified by a short summary, newspaper by newspaper, of the main findings concerning each.

The Daily Papers

(a) The Daily Express

The *Daily Express* is read by one adult in every four. Its readers are distributed fairly evenly amongst every income and age group but it is read rather more by men than by women. Conservatives buy the *Daily Express* more than any other daily paper. About half its readers are Conservative, a quarter Labour sympathizers, and a sixth undecided or non-party. In their leisure interests its readers are similar to any normal group, except that they are rather more than usually interested in sport. On the other hand they are less concerned with their paper's politics than are readers of the *News Chronicle*, a daily paper otherwise with a similar readership group. The *Daily Express* reader tends to prefer a more general, and less politically specialized type of news.

(b) The Daily Mirror

The *Daily Mirror* is read by one adult in every four, particularly by those in the younger and lower-income groups. More than half its readers are Labour supporters, one in seven Conservative, and a quarter are undecided or non-party. As many as one-third of its readers, more than of any other paper, are unaware of the nature of the paper's politics. With readers of the *Daily Graphic*, *Daily Mirror* readers are less interested in *serious news* than readers of any other daily paper; but its simple and lively manner of reporting forms a big part of this paper's attraction. Apart from the news, *Daily Mirror* readers most like the letters and comic strips, and then the pictures. Live Letters and Viewpoint have established themselves very firmly in people's minds as individual features, and are more often referred to by name than any other feature in any other newspaper. Sporting interest is very low.

(c) The Daily Mail

Read by one adult in seven, this is favoured slightly more than the other popular papers by the higher income groups, older people and older women. Just over half its readers are Conservatives, a quarter Labour, and one in seven are undecided or non-party. In comparison with the other three big popular papers, its readers are relatively little interested in politics or 'serious' news, but their sporting interest is on a level with each of the other three. Readers are very interested in feature articles, more so than readers of any other daily paper; 'Don Iddon' is particularly popular.

(d) The Daily Herald

This is read by one adult in eight, particularly men, and with a heavy emphasis on the lower income groups and older Trades Unionists. It has a much bigger one-party majority than any other daily paper: 81 per cent of its readers are Labour supporters, only 10 per cent undecided or non-party, and 7 per cent Conservatives. More than the readers of any other daily paper except the *News Chronicle*, its readers regard it as unbiased and buy it for its politics— although this is very often as much in the broader sense of class as, more specifically, of party politics. News interest is not so strong as it is amongst readers of the *News Chronicle*, *The Times* and the *Daily Telegraph*, but is similar to that of the *Daily Express* and *Daily Mail*. *Daily Herald* readers are probably more interested than readers of any other daily in gambling sports.

(e) The News Chronicle

Read by one adult in every ten, this is equally distributed amongst income groups, but is read rather more amongst men than women and rather more among those over 65. Half its readers are Labour supporters, one-fifth Conservative, one-eighth Liberal, and one-sixth are undecided or non-party. Its readers are more informed about and more interested in 'serious' and political news than readers of any dailies other than *The Times* and the *Daily Telegraph*. Also more than the readers of any daily other than the *Daily Herald*, *News Chronicle* readers buy their paper for its political views, and regard it as unbiased. On the other hand there is a strong sporting component in its readership; with the three other popular dailies it claims more sports enthusiasts than any of the pictorial or 'class' papers. To a striking extent its readership is split between the fairly typical, though Leftish, popular paper reader, and the intellectual minority, more than usually concerned with its political reportage.

(f) The Daily Telegraph

This is read by one adult in sixteen, with a heavy predominance of higher income group and older age group readers. Nearly two-thirds of its readers are Conservatives, 10 per cent Liberals, 9 per cent Labour, and one in six undecided or non-party. Readers of *The Times* and *Daily Telegraph* are more interested in serious news than readers of any other daily paper, and least interested in gambling sports. They are also more inclined to buy the paper for what they feel to be its lack of sensationalism. Letters, and pictures, are barely mentioned by *Daily Telegraph* readers, but feature articles are more popular than in any other paper but the *Daily Mail;* 'Peterborough' is particularly well liked.

(g) The Daily Graphic

One adult in twenty-five reads this paper, women rather more than men and with a marked emphasis on the higher income groups. Just under half its readers are Conservatives, one-quarter Labour, and one-tenth Liberal, while one in six are undecided or non-party.

With the *Daily Mirror*, the other picture paper, *Daily Graphic* readers are less interested in serious news than readers of any other daily, although again they are attracted by this paper's light and easy presentation of the news. Like readers of the *Daily Mirror* and the two 'class' papers they are very little interested in sport. But *Daily Graphic* readers differ from readers of the *Daily Mirror* in their Right-wing inclinations, and also in giving first preference to pictures rather than to letters and comics. Even so they enjoy the letters more than readers of any other daily but the *Daily Mirror*.

(h) The Times

The Times is read by one adult in fifty, and with a very pronounced emphasis on the older and higher income groups. Two-fifths of its readers are Conservatives, one-quarter Labour, one in eight Liberal, and one-fifth undecided or non-party. Because of its small circulation our sample contained too few *Times* readers to portray them adequately, but there are many indications to suggest that they are very similar to readers of the *Daily Telegraph*, in their pronounced interest in news, for instance, in their liking for unsensational reportage, and in their almost total lack of interest in sport and pictures. Their chief difference lies in their less pronouncedly Conservative politics.

(i) The Daily Worker

This is read by fewer than 1 per cent of all adults, so that it has remained, unfortunately, almost totally outside our scope in this survey.

The Sunday Papers

(a) The News of the World

This paper is read by *every second adult*, and is especially popular amongst people of the unskilled working-class. In spite of its Conservative sympathies, just over half the readers of this paper are Labour supporters, and only one-quarter Conservatives, and one-fifth undecided or non-party. Instead of the concentration of interest on single exclusive feature articles, characteristic of readers of most other popular Sunday papers, the *News of the World* readers are most of all interested in gossip and scandal news; as many as two-fifths admit this quite freely. In addition, sporting interest is stronger here than in any other Sunday paper. Feature articles, on the other hand, constitute an attraction for very few of its readers, and the very low level of interest in serious news can be seen in the fact that the majority of the *News of the World* readers are buying a paper whose editorial politics come into direct conflict with their own.

(b) The People

Read by one adult in three, this newspaper is fairly evenly distributed amongst the income groups. Half its readers are Labour supporters, one-quarter Conservatives, and one-fifth undecided or non-party. Its readers are second only to those of the *News of the World* in their admitted interest in news of a gossip and scandal type; readers of these two Sunday papers alone voluntarily *admit* their interest in this sort of news. Sporting interest is strong among readers of *The People*. Interest in feature articles is divided amongst, particularly, Hannen Swaffer, Helliwell, 'Man of the People' and Lyndoe.

(c) The Sunday Pictorial

Readers of the *Sunday Pictorial* form a quarter of all adults, and are drawn fairly evenly from most groups, though with an emphasis on younger readers. Just over half are Labour supporters, a fifth are Conservatives, and a quarter are undecided or non-party. Sporting interest is pronounced, being on a level with that of the *News of the World* and the *People*, but interest in serious news is relatively infrequent. The main attraction of this paper is, naturally, the pictures; nearly half its readers say this is what they particularly like. Interest in feature articles is average for Sunday papers, but shows the characteristic tendency to concentrate on one only; at the time of this survey this was the series 'The Birth of a Baby'.

(d) The Sunday Express

This is read by one adult in five, and particularly by the better-off. With the *News of the World*, this is the Sunday paper most read by

Conservatives. Just over half its readers are Conservative sympathizers, a quarter support Labour, and one in ten is undecided
or non-party. After the *Sunday Times*, the *Observer* and *Reynolds
News*, readers of the *Sunday Express* are most of all interested in
serious news, and best informed about it. Their interest in sport, on
the other hand, is lower than that of any Sunday readership group
but the *Observer* and *Sunday Times*. Alone of all Sunday paper
readers, letters and comics (both verbal and graphic) are a strong
attraction. Nat Gubbins and Giles are particularly popular. But
feature articles are the biggest draw; nearly half our *Sunday Express*
informants mentioned their liking for these and, characteristically of
Sunday paper readers, their interest tended to concentrate on one
series alone; at the time of the survey this was the Duke of Windsor's
autobiography.

(e) The Sunday Dispatch

One adult in eight reads this paper, particularly members of the
higher income groups. Half its readers are Conservatives, one in
three Labour supporters, and one in ten are undecided or non-
party. General news interest amongst them is average for Sunday
papers, although interest in sports news is on a high level. But
readers of the *Sunday Dispatch* have few outstanding characteristics
of their own. On the whole their one peculiarity is that they pay
relatively little attention (for Sunday paper readers) to feature
articles, making up for this with their interest in the weekly serial
story.

(f) The Sunday Graphic

One adult in fourteen reads the *Sunday Graphic*, especially the
better-off. Just over half its readers are Conservatives, one-fifth are
Labour supporters, one-eighth Liberals, and a similar proportion
politically undecided or non-party. Its readers appear to be more or
less unconcerned with 'serious' news, although they also pay relatively
little attention to gossip and scandal. Sports news is almost entirely
a matter of indifference to them, and also letters and comics. Easily

the biggest draw are the pictures, mentioned by more than half this group of readers as an outstanding attraction to them. Not even *Sunday Pictorial* readers are so exclusively interested in pictures; and feature articles, the great Sunday attraction, are in this case considerably less popular.

(g) Reynolds News

This is read by one in twenty-three of all adults: it is particularly popular amongst men, but evenly distributed amongst all income groups. More than the readers of any other Sunday paper this readership group is confined to one political outlook; two-thirds are Labour supporters, about one in ten Communist, with only one in fourteen Conservative and one in seven undecided or non-party. Moreover this is the only Sunday paper explicitly enjoyed by a large-sized group of its readers specifically for its political views. With readers of the *Observer* and *Sunday Times*, *Reynolds News* readers are more interested than any other Sunday readership group in serious news; and, although readers of *Reynolds News* show a high level of sports interest, few of them feel their concern with the sports page to be a major interest. Similarly, their *relative* degree of interest in feature articles is below average, and they tend not to be exclusively concerned with any single feature series.

(h) The Sunday Times

Read by one in twenty-five of all adults, readers of this paper are very largely drawn from the higher income groups. Just over half are Conservatives, and similar proportions, one-sixth, are Liberal and Labour: just over one in ten are undecided and non-party. Its readers are little interested in gambling sports, but pronouncedly concerned with serious news; with readers of *Reynolds News* and the *Observer*, they emerge at the highest level of Sunday news interest. They are very interested in feature articles, mentioned by just over half as something that they particularly like; reviews are particularly popular.

(i) The Observer

One adult in thirty-three reads the *Observer* on Sundays, again with a heavy preponderance of the financially well-off. Just over two-fifths of its readers are Conservatives, one-fifth Labour supporters, one-sixth Liberal and one-eighth undecided or non-party. Except for this rather smaller proportion of Conservatives, *Observer* readers are very similar to those of the *Sunday Times*. Like them they are very interested in serious news, and relatively indifferent to sport. Like them, too, they are most of all concerned with the feature articles, although this time more so. As many as two-thirds of all our sample of *Observer* readers said they particularly liked the feature articles; again reviews played an important part in these. But on the whole the two papers can be distinguished one from the other not only by the rather stronger Right-wing tendency of *Sunday Times* readers, but also by their more pronounced preoccupation with news and political reportage at the expense, to some extent, of feature articles and reviews.

APPENDIX I

Sources

THE present survey is by no means the first venture into the newspaper field. The Hulton Readership Surveys of 1947 and 1948, for instance, have made exhaustive studies of the extent to which the bigger papers and periodicals are read as well as delineating the groups into which their readers fall. Mass-Observation's own survey makes no attempt to cover the same ground over again. Instead it was planned and carried on the basis of the 1947 Hulton Readership Survey and wherever the present report makes reference to absolute readership figures they are almost always derived from this.

Our own aim has been the much less purely statistical one of discovering just why people read newspapers, how far they are influenced by them, and exactly how they feel about what they read. A subsidiary task was to investigate differences between the readerships of the various newspapers, not so much in respect of objective criteria such as sex, age, class, etc., as in their less easily definable differences of interest, outlook, attitude and even temperament. For all this it was necessary to supplement statistics with material of a more qualitative type, likely to throw light on such problems of depth and feeling. Working along these lines our own material has been accumulated by employing a number of different techniques in each of several separate but parallel and integrated investigations. It falls into the following groups:

A: DIRECT QUESTIONING

(1) The basic survey consisted of 1,600 interviews made during the period November 1947 to March 1948, on a regional sample. Questions were framed to discover not only which papers people read and how they feel about them, but also to get, for correlation purposes, a detailed picture of the contacts' interests, outlook, and attitudes. Of these, 900 interviews were designed purely on a cross-off, factual basis, and 700 additionally elicited

more detailed attitudinal replies which were recorded verbatim. They were distributed amongst:

Putney	Birmingham
Croydon	Bristol
Tottenham	Essex Villages
Hendon	Bolton

200 interviews were made in each of the London districts and 150 in each of the others. Of the 800 London interviews altogether 300 were of the more detailed verbatim type, whilst in each of the other areas 100 of the total 150 were attitudinal ones.

The verbatim attitudinal interviews were based on the results of the 1947 Hulton Readership Survey, in that the sample was constructed so as to obtain correctly proportioned numbers reading each of the national dailies. The sample for the remaining—and purely factual—900 interviews was made representative of the population as a whole in respect of sex, age, and income group.

(2) In addition to this, further questions (with subdivisions) were put into a second questionnaire. This consisted of 1,000 interviews, again made on a regional rather than a national basis, and asked during April 1948. These were designed to test the influence of newspapers on their readers—in respect of the formation of political opinion, long-term and short-term, on cinema going, and in the filling in of football pools. The sample was stratified according to social class and age (based on figures published by the Registrar-General).

(3) Small-scale surveys (100 interviews each) were made in October 1947 on daily paper and Sunday paper reading. Interviewing in this case was in London only. Interviews were very long and detailed and were designed to get a general picture of newspaper reading within the family.

(4) Five hundred interviews were made during the Gravesend By-election in 1947, relating newspaper reading to voting intentions and voting background.

(5) Re-analysis of material from earlier surveys, for the purpose of extracting information relevant to newspapers; notably a 1946 investigation into reading habits in Tottenham and a 1947 national sample survey of book reading. The Tottenham survey consisted of 1,000 interviews carried out with inhabitants of Tottenham, their names and addresses being extracted from Food Office returns in such a way as to constitute a statistically random sample. The book reading survey was made regionally and consisted of 1,000 interviews, representative in respect of sex, age and social class of the population as a whole.

(6) With the co-operation of schoolteachers, about 250 schoolboys and schoolgirls, between the ages of 10 and 16, were questioned about the newspapers they usually saw, what they liked to read in them and why.

119

SOURCES

B: PENETRATIVE MATERIAL

All the foregoing material was obtained by the use of formal questionnaires. To supplement this, one of our biggest sources of penetrative material was Mass-Observation's National Panel of voluntary observers.[1]

(1) Panel members were asked questions in 1942, 1946 and 1947 on the daily newspapers they read and their attitudes to them. This included, in 1947, a test designed to discover which newspaper items had made the biggest impact on readers and questions inviting detailed accounts of how and when the paper is read, which parts of it, and why.

(2) In July 1947 a question was asked concerning Sunday papers read, and covering similar points to those of the 1947 question on daily newspaper reading.

(3) In September 1947 the same group was asked about its habits in respect of local paper reading, and attitudes to them.

C: OBSERVATIONAL MATERIAL

(1) Follows of people were made buying papers, observing when they were read, which parts, in what order, and for how long.

(2) Observations in public libraries were made, noting the time spent on each item in each paper, and the order of reading, etc.

(3) Observation of buying at newsagents was carried out, and informal conversations with the newsagents themselves.

D: BACKGROUND MATERIAL

Extensive use was also made of material collected by Mass-Observation in previous surveys, including the *Daily Telegraph* survey on Capital Punishment which involved 6,000 interviews.

---

[1] Mass-Observation's National Panel of voluntary observers, a nation-wide and predominantly middle-class group, above average in education and intelligence, and more than usually socially minded. This group sends in long and detailed written replies to questions sent to them every month; and much of their value lies not only in the factual reliability of their information, but also in the extent to which they are able to analyse and express their feelings on less factual subjects.

APPENDIX II
Advertisement Appeal

How much notice do readers take of the advertisements in the newspaper? Our survey suggests that although conscious interest in advertisements appears to be low, their practical impact is considerably stronger.

In our national sample survey, for instance, only 4 per cent of the people asked what they read in their daily paper mentioned the advertisements—and only 6 per cent said they never read them at all. It is clear that people are not consciously, or lastingly, interested in advertisements themselves. Yet later in the questionnaire the same people were asked if they could remember any newspaper advertisements specifically for cigarettes, tobacco, drinks, skirts or aeroplane travel,[1] and they were given the further opportunity to specify the name of maker, brand and shop. *Only about two-fifths of the whole daily paper-reading group could specify none, and most of the rest mentioned three or more;* Table 41 relates newspaper reading to the number of types of advertisement seen.

Quite clearly, people read advertisements and for the most part are able to recall them *when reminded*. It is interesting that the level of conscious interest is lowest amongst readers of the more working-class dailies. Nearly half the readers of both *Daily Mirror* and *Daily Herald* can remember no advertisements (of these specified types) at all, whereas at the opposite extreme more than half the readers of *The Times*, and nearly half the readers of the *Daily Mail*, can recall from four to six different types of advertisement. But this does not mean that working-class readers are influenced by advertisements less than the middle-classes; ability to recall advertisements is one thing—the subconscious assimilation of their lesson may be quite another matter.

[1] These products were chosen arbitrarily.

TABLE 41

Percentage of people reading these DAILIES who can recall this number of newspaper advertisements[1]:

Number of Adverts. Recalled	Daily Express %	Daily Mail %	Daily Mirror %	Daily Herald %	News Chronicle %	Daily Telegraph %	Daily Graphic %
0	38	27	46	46	41	32	33
1	8	5	5	7	4	5	5
2	8	13	9	9	8	12	10
3	14	9	9	10	9	14	15
4	10	18	9	11	11	12	17
5	10	16	13	10	16	7	8
6	12	12	9	7	11	18	12

[1] People were asked only about the six types of products specified. If they mentioned two kinds of any types of product, e.g. two brands of cigarettes, this was only counted as one *for the purpose of this table*. For this reason no one could be coded as having remembered more than six types of advertisement.

TABLE 42

Percentage of advertisements of these types, seen by men and women, referring to each of these products:

	Men %	Women %	Total %
Tobacco	17	12	15
Cigarettes	21	19	20
Drink	21	18	20
Biscuits	16	20	18
Skirts	11	23	16
Air travel	14	8	11

Sex differences in the *number* of advertisements remembered are negligible; in the *kinds* of advertisement remembered, on the other hand, there is a slight variation: see Table 42.

Results fall into the standard sex pattern. Feminine interest in rations and clothes leads women to pay relatively more attention than men to advertisements for biscuits and skirts. People evidently tend to remember chiefly advertisements for a product in which they have a special interest. But again, of course, this does not necessarily mean that they allow their advertisement reading to guide their buying.

All our material, in fact, only serves to show the need for extensive further research on the subject of advertising. It is necessary to define the relation between unconscious assimilation and conscious recollections; to outline the process by which advertisements exercise their underground influence, and, finally to discover the extent to which all this is related to buying the product advertised. Our material can attempt no more than a very rough and inadequate indication of the problems to be solved; the next stage in research will need more subtle and penetrative methods than those we have been able to employ for this preliminary survey.

APPENDIX III: TABLES

(General Note: Throughout the following tables reference to The Times has been omitted due to the small number of readers of this paper contained in Mass-Observation's sample. Particular care should also be taken in considering the figures given for other newspapers with comparatively small circulations, e.g. Daily Graphic, Sunday Times, the Observer.)

TABLE 43

Percentage of people reading these Daily Papers who say that these are the main things they like about it:

	Daily Express %	Daily Mirror %	Daily Mail %	Daily Herald %	News Chronicle %	Daily Telegraph %	Daily Graphic %	Total %
News	35	17	26	25	21	47	15	27
Gossip, etc.	1	1	4	2	1	3	—	2
Sport	20	2	12	18	22	—	6	12
Comics, cartoons	7	27	7	1	4	16	3	10
Feature articles	9	5	22	14	14	10	—	10
Editorial	11	3	12	4	17	3	9	10
Letters	1	29	1	4	3	16	12	9
Political line	6	3	9	21	24	—	3	8
Pictures	1	18	1	—			32	6
Vague, generally approving	27	16	22	18	25	23	23	22
Miscellaneous	4	6	5	5	4	9	9	5
Don't know	5	6	3	12	3	3	9	5

(N.B.—Percentages add to more than 100 because many people mention more than one item.)

TABLE 44

Percentage of people reading these Sunday Papers who say that these are the main things they like about it:

	News of the World %	The People %	Sunday Pictorial %	Sunday Express %	Sunday Dispatch %	Sunday Graphic %	Reynolds News %	Sunday Times %	The Observer %	Total %
News	26	18	17	18	22	22	9	13	21	21
Gossip, etc.	41	14	1	1	2	—	—	—	3	15
Sport	17	14	12	8	20	—	4	9	3	13
Comics, cartoons	—	—	1	13	2	33	—	—	—	2
Feature articles	5	32	27	40	20	1	17	52	69	24
Editorial	1	7	3	5	2	—	4	22	3	4
Letters	2	—	—	13	2	—	—	—	—	3
Political angle	—	2	5	5	4	—	17	9	7	3
Pictures	—	2	45	4	4	53	—	—	—	7
Vague, generally approving	12	13	9	19	22	6	22	17	14	14
Miscellaneous	17	18	10	4	24	6	13	30	14	15
Don't know	4	6	1	3	12	11	9	—	3	9

TABLE 45

Percentage of people reading these Daily Papers who support these Parties:

Party	Daily Express %	Daily Mirror %	Daily Mail %	Daily Herald %	News Chronicle %	Daily Telegraph %	Daily Graphic %
Support none, undecided	17	24	15	10	17	17	18
Labour	28	58	26	81	50	9	26
Conservative	48	15	51	7	19	62	46
Liberal	5	2	6	2	12	10	10
Other	2	1	2	—	2	2	—

TABLE 46

Percentage of people reading these SUNDAY papers who say they support these political parties

	News of the World %	The People %	Sunday Pictorial %	Sunday Express %	Sunday Dispatch %	Sunday Graphic %	Reynolds News %	Sunday Times %	The Observer %	Read None %
Support none, uninterested	20	19	23	12	12	12	14	12	13	29
Labour	53	49	52	28	36	22	65	17	22	33
Conservative	23	25	20	53	47	53	7	54	44	29
Liberal	2	5	4	6	2	13	1	17	18	9
Other	2	2	1	1	3	—	13	—	3	—

TABLE 47

Percentage of readers of these DAILY papers, with this conception of their paper's politics:

Party supported	Daily Express %	Daily Mirror %	Daily Mail %	Daily Herald %	News Chronicle %	Daily Telegraph %	Daily Graphic %
None	3	6	2	1	4	3	10
Conservative	70	5	67	4	9	83	52
Liberal	2	1	2	1	47	3	—
Labour	4	55	7	79	20	—	24
Communist	—	1	—	1	—	—	—
Independent	3	1	2	—	—	—	—
Don't know	18	31	20	14	20	11	14

TABLE 48

*Number of people who are unfriendly to America for every 100 who
are friendly amongst readers of these Daily papers:*

Daily Herald	34
News Chronicle	26
Daily Graphic	23
Daily Express	22
Daily Mirror	21
Daily Mail	17
Daily Telegraph	1

TABLE 49

*Number of people who are unfriendly to Russia for every 100 who
are friendly amongst readers of these Daily papers:*

Daily Mail	220
Daily Telegraph	196
Daily Graphic	172
Daily Express	166
News Chronicle	124
Daily Mirror	93
Daily Herald	83

TABLE 50

*Number of people who are unfriendly to America for every 100 who
are friendly amongst readers of these Sunday papers:*

Reynolds News	67
The People	31
News of the World	25
Sunday Pictorial	24
Sunday Dispatch	17
Sunday Express	16
Sunday Times	11
Observer	6
Sunday Graphic	3

TABLE 51

Number of people who are unfriendly to Russia for every 100 who are friendly amongst readers of these Sunday papers:

Sunday Times	171
Sunday Express	143
Observer	137
Sunday Dispatch	132
The People	131
Sunday Pictorial	118
News of the World	117
Sunday Graphic	96
Reynolds News	22

Printed and bound by CPI Group (UK) Ltd, Croydon, CR0 4YY

06/01/2025

01815878-0004